Reef Fishes of the Red Sea

A Guide to Identification

Richard and Mary Field

KEGAN PAUL INTERNATIONAL
LONDON AND NEW YORK

First published in 1998 by
Kegan Paul International
UK: P.O. Box 256, London WC1B 3SW, England
Tel: (0171) 580 5511 Fax: (0171) 436 0899
E-mail: books@keganpau.demon.co.uk
Internet: http://www.demon.co.uk/keganpaul/
USA: 562 West 113th Street, New York, NY, 10025, USA
Tel: (212) 666 1000 Fax: (212) 316 3100

Distributed by
John Wiley & Sons Ltd
Southern Cross Trading Estate
1 Oldlands Way, Bognor Regis
West Sussex, PO22 9SA, England
Tel: (01243) 779 777 Fax: (01243) 820 250

Columbia University Press
562 West 113th Street
New York, NY 10025, USA
Tel: (212) 666 1000 Fax: (212) 316 3100

Set in Sabon

Printed in Great Britain by The Bath Press

British Library Cataloguing in Publication Data

Field, Richard
Reef Fishes of the Red Sea
1. Coral reef fishes - Red Sea - Identification
I. Title II. Field, Mary
597'.0916533
ISBN 0-7103-0613-X
A catalogue record for this book is available from the British Library

Library of Congress Cataloging-in-Publication Data
A catalogue record for this book is available from the Library of Congress

Acknowledgements

We wish to express our sincere gratitude to the following companies whose generous support has enabled us to complete this book:

Saudi Binladin Group

Saudi Arabian Airlines

The authors wish to acknowledge the help of the Natural History Museum in London, and in particular Dr. Anthony Gill, Senior Scientific Officer, who helped us with some very useful advice and also allowed us to use the Fish Section Library.

We also wish to thank the staff of the University of Toronto, who allowed us access to its considerable resources, and also the Library of the Royal Ontario Museum for allowing access to information on fishes.

Our thanks go to our son Francis, who has made a valuable contribution in the form of photographs, drawings and comment, and who has provided a sharp pair of eyes on our dives together.

Contents

Introduction

The Red Sea

One of life's mysteries is the origin of the name of this bluest of all seas. There have been many plausible suggestions, but very little to substantiate them. The most favoured is associated with the rapid growth and consequent demise of the population of a particular planktonic algae. The result of this cyclic phenomenon is a floating red/brown scum, which under certain light conditions gives the appearance of a strip of red carpet spread across the Sea.

The first, and only, time when we witnessed this event on a large scale, off Port Sudan in 1964, the origin of the name Red Sea immediately occurred to me. On that occasion, the 'red tide' stretched for miles eastward towards Jeddah, as a broad red band.

A second explanation is attributed to the preponderance of the beautiful red Anthias fish seen along the fringing reefs. Certain sponges of a scarlet colour may also be seen in these areas contributing to the overall perception of red.

There is of course a third explanation which follows from the frequent red sunset skies, enhanced by airborne reddish dust.

No clues to origin are suggested by earlier names, in other languages - the arabic name is a straight translation from the English. Previous arabic names do not, as far as is known, include a reference to colour.

As a sea, the Red Sea is relatively small in area - however, with a central depth of 3040m it contains a massive amount of water compared to other small seas. It's origins go back some 20 million years ago when a split occurred along the central rift - the coastal divide continues to widen to this day, at a rate estimated to be 1.2cm per year. It is now known that there is considerable volcanic activity along the central rift, which must make the deep sea bed a very turbulent area.

To the amateur diver or snorkeller, visiting an outer reef or simply swimming offshore, the Red Sea would appear to have an abundance of fish and a huge variety of species. What he sees however, are small highly concentrated population areas, that do not represent the Sea as a whole. In fact the Sea is probably underpopulated, since the basic prerequisites for abundant and replenishable fish stock are somewhat limited.

Animal life in the sea is ultimately supported, at the bottom of the food chain, by the presence of nutrient salts. These salts enable plankton growth under photosynthesis, which in turn provides a continuing source of essential food for marine animal survival.

The usual main sources for nutrient salts are river outflows, which the Red Sea lacks. The nutrient salt supply from coastal sources is therefore minimal. Salts can also be distributed from more fertile areas by oceanic currents. The Red Sea is virtually enclosed, and it seems unlikely that incoming currents alone could support a high planktonic concentration.

However, the Red Sea does enjoy an abundance of sunlight, clear water and warm temperatures down to a considerable depth, which suggests that planktonic growth is more efficient than in many other seas and that recycling of salts is accomplished effectively. Perhaps the absence of river outflows and oceanic currents, with their inevitable malign chemicals from man-made products, allows for a greater efficiency.

Water movement in the Sea is aided by the cooling effect of high evaporation resulting from the constant breezes - a snorkeller can testify to the sometimes dramatic and breathtaking changes in temperature in the shallower areas of reef. The usually large expanse of shallow water between shoreline and fringing reef can cool very rapidly in a strong dry northerly wind, thereby causing heavy water flow over the reef and into the depths.

The implication from the physical circumstances of the Red Sea's existence is that fish life is heavily concentrated around and within the coral reefs, and that the Sea does not support a huge population in relation to its parent, the Indian Ocean. It would also seem that, when the variety of known species is compared to the variety found in the Indian Ocean, there are much fewer species than could be expected, and that over the period of the Red Sea's existence, the survival of species has been of a very ordered nature.

It is plain to deduce, that if the Red Sea is to maintain its magnificence, the highly efficient production of plankton must be maintained - factors directly affecting that efficiency are principally sunlight, water movement, clarity and cleanliness. Any change in these parameters will cause a change in the balance of life in the Sea.

The Red Sea owes much of its character to the surrounding terrain of mostly desert regions. Salinity is generally high but varies along the length of the Sea - it is highest in the north, lowest in the south. This characteristic may well account for the different concentrations of various species of fish. Some species may not have been able to adapt to a higher salinity, thereby explaining their absence from the Red Sea and presence in the Indian Ocean. The lower salinity of the southern part of the Red Sea appears to be more suitable for the large schools of commercially exploitable pelagic fish that are found there, but not in the central and northern reaches.

Richard and Mary Field
Jeddah, November 1997

Scope of this book

This book is primarily a guide to the identification of the most frequently seen reef fishes in the Red Sea. It is intended to be a photographic reference book, not one to be displayed on the coffee table. All the photographs, without exception, shown in this book were taken of fish in the Red Sea by the authors and their son. In some cases, fish were removed from the Sea to the author's aquarium, specifically to be photographed.

Fish species in the Red Sea are generally spread unevenly throughout the Sea. In one area a particular species may be plentiful, whilst a 100 miles away it will be absent. Similarly, in different areas some species are found at different depths.

The various authors of books on the subject of Red Sea fishes disagree on the distribution of some species - in this book, references to the densities of population of the various species are specific to the middle section of the Red Sea, along the Saudi Arabian coastline. Although some photographs were taken off the Egyptian north east coast, the great majority are from this region, along the coastline and amongst the outer reefs up to 20 miles offshore.

Many common Red Sea species are not included since they cannot strictly be called reef fishes. Amongst these are the Cartilagenous fishes (Sharks, Rays) and the truly pelagic, such as Tuna, Jacks and the other 'sports fishing' species. Although these fishes may be to a greater or lesser extent dependent on the reef fauna for their survival, they do not permanently inhabit the reef, but may visit to sleep or forage; however, a small number of photographs are included of very commonly seen fishes in this category - these are of the Stingrays and the most common Jacks, Barracudas and Mackerels, shown in the chapter on Open Water Fishes.

Some of the descriptions of fishes are somewhat anthropomorphic, and would therefore be considered unscientific by experts. This book is intended for divers and snorkellers who observe the fishes of the Red Sea as a relaxing pastime, and who wish to identify what they see. A whimsical description of a species can often be a more useful aid to identification than details of scales, spines and teeth expressed in scientific language.

It is customary in scientific books to depict fishes with all their spines erect and tail spread - in its natural habitat, a fish is seldom seen like this (with the exception perhaps of Cardinalfishes). What the recreational diver and snorkeller sees are colours, patterns, swimming action and, strangely, eyes. These are the characteristics used in this book to assist in the identification of fishes.

However, every effort has been made to ensure that identifications are accurate, and that the latest accepted names are used. There is still much work to be done by the scientific community in agreeing classifications and naming of Red Sea fishes - the names used in this book, in some cases, may differ from those in others, which simply shows the extent of uncertainty.

The section of this book describing the various families of fishes is arranged primarily according to Order (names of Orders end in ***-iformes***) within which the family occurs - most fishes described are in the Order Perciformes; families in this Order are listed alphabetically by common name.

The authors have had considerable difficulty in identifying some juvenile forms of Red Sea fishes - Parrotfishes are amongst the most difficult. Juvenile forms and colours of Red Sea fishes have not been documented fully in either scientific or popular publications. The only sure way to identify juveniles is to capture them (not an easy task) and have an expert examine them. In some cases, the authors, in desperation, have captured juveniles and resorted to observing their development into another, recognisable, stage within the confines of an aquarium. This can be a lengthy process!

There are many small fishes, typically Gobies and Blenny-like creatures, that will be seen in the Red Sea, if the observer is patient and curious enough to examine the contents of coral branches, sponges and gorgonions (or even sea cucumbers!). Very little data is available on these species - perhaps now that macro photography is possible underwater, these tiny creatures will receive the attention of marine zoologists. Such fishes are not fully covered by this book - we hope that some day a book will be written describing these often beautiful little animals.

There are a number of species which are not recorded in this book, despite being present in the Red Sea - within the text at the beginning of each chapter describing the various families, a figure is given for the number of species in the family that are reported to exist in the Red Sea. This figure is taken from 'CLOFRES II ; An Updated Checklist of Fishes of the Red Sea' dated 1994. At the end of each chapter there is a list which includes only those species which have to date been documented in popular publications.

The number of species currently considered to be endemic to the Red Sea is 171 - this represents some 13.7% of the total number of species known to inhabit the Red Sea. Some of the species listed may only be seen in specific areas, such as the Gulf of Aqaba or the extreme south of the Red Sea, so not all will have a companion photograph.

Some of the photographs in this book were taken of specimens in the authors' aquarium, an example of which is that of the Longfin, *P. nigricans*. This specimen was temporarily captured solely to photograph it, and was returned to the sea immediately afterwards. Such a species is very difficult to photograph in its preferred natural environment, which in this case, was a sea grass bed in turbid and very shallow (10cm)water.

Reef Profile

1 **Shallow lagoon area inside the reef - depth to 2m**

Often a sandy bottom, with isolated coral heads and/or seagrass beds; this area contains many reef fish juveniles of many species, most of which will migrate to the fringing reef as they mature. The coral heads contain communities composed of a variety of reef fishes, some adult, some juvenile.

The sandy areas contain a resident population of bottom dwellers, which includes Flounders and Soles, Gobies, and Snake Eels. There are also free swimming resident species, typically Monos, Mojarras and Rabbitfishes which are often caught by shore anglers. These, however, are not the only possible reward for anglers - the lagoon area will often be visited by large predatory species in foraging parties. Jacks will often go close inshore to feed. An early morning visit to a lagoon area may also provide an opportunity to see a huge school of resting Barracuda close inshore.

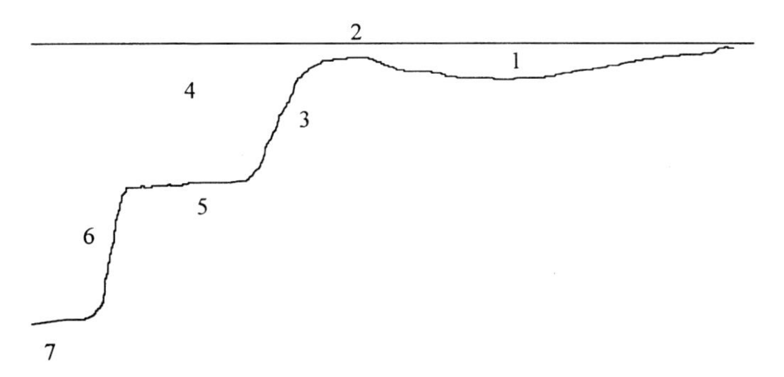

2 **Fringing reef**

The often turbulent water over the fringing reef is home to a great variety of reef fishes. The Sohal Surgeonfish is a dominant resident of this area, with certain Damselfishes exercising their own dominance over small patches of territory. Here large Broomtail Wrasses and Parrotfishes will be seen amongst the plethora of small fish. Chestnut Blennies will be scurrying from crevice to crevice watched perhaps by the ever-present Stocky Hawkfishes. All together a very busy place.

3 **Reef face**

The area with the greatest variety of species from amongst all the common reef fishes eg. Anthias, Damselfishes, small Groupers, Butterflyfishes, Angelfishes, Porcupinefishes, Squirrelfishes, Sweepers and Cardinalfishes in crevices; Cornetfishes; Lionfish under ledges and at the bottom of the reef, Moray eels, Pufferfishes and Trunkfishes.

4 **Shallow open water**

Larger fishes such as Snappers, Chub, Emperors, Tuna, Jacks, and Barracuda; shoaling fish such as Redtooth Triggerfishes, Fusiliers, Mackerel.

5 **First shelf**
Usually at about 15-20m; sandy with coral outcrops or rocks - Goatfishes, larger Groupers, Parrotfish, Chromis in coral heads, Rockmover Wrasses, burrowing or well-camouflaged fishes such as Gobies, Quakerfishes, Stonefishes, Crocodile fishes.

6 **Second reef face**
Similar to area 3 but with less light, there is less coral and fewer species of fish - larger Angelfishes such as Yellowbar, Arabian; Yellowface Soapfishes and Squirrelfishes.

7 **Second shelf**
30-40m; coral debris swept down from above, very little or no live hard coral but large sponges; contains deeper water species such as Zebra Angelfish, Longnose Hawkfish.

A note on observing fishes

For snorkellers and divers alike, the first early morning look over the fringing reef, or under the boat, can be the most rewarding moment of the day. To be first over the reef is to be the first to see the larger fishes that rule during the quiet night. Once disturbed these fishes will quickly disappear and not be seen again during the day. It is well worthwhile to enter the water gently, or approach a reef cautiously, to catch a glimpse of life in the sea as it is without the presence of humans.

When a diver starts his descent, he should look around, before the rays, turtles and other larger creatures decide to escape his intrusion into their world. When entering the water from a boat, a clumsy entry can frighten away the very animals that the diver wishes to see!

To be carefully approaching a large pod of Dolphins for the photograph of a lifetime, and have a fellow diver launch himself, flat finned and flailing, into the water above is an occasion for reconsidering friendships.

At the beginning of a dive, we have adopted the practice of gently descending to 10-15m, preferrably just above the second reef face, and then we keep quite still for a few minutes - by doing this, we have experienced large fishes coming close to investigate us. This is a simple, and very rewarding habit.

Divers should always move carefully in the water, and particularly when investigating the contents of a coral head or other hiding place. Although it is contrary to good diving practice to hold one's breath, as long as one is relaxed and maintaining the same level, it is sometimes acceptable and necessary when approaching fish - particularly when taking photographs. Bubbles can frighten fish, not only because they can be seen, but because they have noisy origins! The sea is already a noisy place, but to introduce an unfamiliar sound may make an interesting subject quickly dart for cover.

When we are taught to drive a car we are told to be aware of what is around us - the same rule applies to diving - it is all too easy to become absorbed, and so miss the shark that everyone else saw!

At night many fish sleep, and they can be observed very closely. When using a torch, project the beam to one side of the fish, and preferrably use a narrow beam torch. Light will confuse and frighten them, and they will not swim directly into your torch beam.

When observing fishes in the water, the diver should be aware that the colours that he sees may not be the same as those that he sees in photographs. The sea acts as a blue filter, so that colours at the opposite end of the spectrum, such as red, cannot be seen at depth. Perhaps the best example of a fish that demonstrates this effect is the Orchid Dottyback which in daylight is orchid coloured, but at its usual depth of about 10-20m it appears blue. A photograph taken at depth with flash, of course, restores the missing colours. The colour red is quite a dominant colour in fishes, which may help them to hide at depth - although I have often wondered whether the colour perception of man can be compared with that of fishes.

The sizing of species has been a problem for the authors. The various publications on Red Sea fishes do not unfortunately always agree on the length of fishes. The authors have therefore not attempted to specify the maximum size of every species (can a scientist or amateur claim to have caught and measured the largest fish of a species?), but has included general statements in the text on the various families, and has included with each photograph an estimate of the greatest length likely to be seen.

Judging the size of fishes in the water is not always easy, since the observer sees refracted images that make a subject appear closer than it actually is - so what may appear to be a 2m long Barracuda will actually be 1.6m!

Whilst a diver observes, he can be sure that many eyes observe him. Fish below a diver are able to quite clearly see shapes against the sunlit background, whilst remaining unseen in the gloomy depths. It should not go unnoticed that most of the non-pelagic fishes are dark coloured on top of their body and, usually, silver or white coloured on the underside. This is of course effective camouflage, and makes some of those large bottom dwelling fish very difficult to see.

Notes on the naming of fishes

Scientific names are made up of two parts. The first part is the name of the Genus (generic name) and the second the Species (specific name). The generic name always begins with an upper case letter, the specific name with lower case. eg. *Arusetta asfur* (Arabian angelfish).

A genus contains animals that are very closely related in terms of outward appearance (morphology), internal structure (anatomy) and reproductive habits. Members of the same genus are usually very similar in shape and size but they will differ in colour and small details such as the shape of the tail, number of teeth and so on. A genus can have many members - eg. the genus *Chaetodon,* a major genus of Butterflyfishes contains more than 60 species world wide. On the other end of the scale the genus *Bolbometopon* contains only one species, *Bolbomethopon muricatum,* the Bumphead Parrotfish.

The strict biological definition of a species is a group of organisms that reproduce sexually to produce fertile offspring. Members of a genus may be able to interbreed but the offspring will always be sterile.

The genus and species together define a unique animal. At times a third name is added to specify a local variant of a species. The Red Sea variant of the Vermiculate Wrasse has been named by Randall as *Macropharyngodon bipartitus marisrubri.*

The scientific names of animals are consistent throughout the world. Whatever variations there are result from disagreements amongst biologists as to which group certain animals belong to. The characteristics used in classification overlap to a great degree and it is not always easy to decide at what point the differences become great enough to warrant the introduction of a new genus or species. Confusion also arises as a result of the same animal having been found and named by different people in different parts of the world. In the case of some fish different names have arisen for species that have a juvenile phase that looks very different from the adult. Reference books usually quote the name of the discoverer and the date after the scientific name. The rule is that the oldest published name should prevail - this, however, is easier to state than apply. A typical example of confusion surrounds the Arabian Angelfish, which is placed in the genus *Arusetta* by Carcasson and also Allen, *Pomacanthus* by Randall and Debelius and finally *Euxiphipops* by Wheeler. In his latest book, Coastal Fishes of Oman, Randall has adopted *Arusetta* genus.

Scientific names are often derived from Latin or sometimes Greek words that describe a particular feature of the fish. Turkeyfish are in the genus *Pterois* from the Greek word for 'wing' (to be doubly sure, the W Australian form of *P. miles* is *Pterois volitans* which has both latin and greek origins!). The pectoral wings of the Lionfish and Turkeyfish are indeed reminiscent of wings as the fish gently glides through the water. The genus *Chaetodon* of the Butterflyfish family is named after the brush-like teeth of its members.

Specific names are more varied in origin being derived from appearance (eg. *Paracheilinus octotaenia* - Eightline Wrasse), the name of the discoverer (*Thalassoma klunzingeri* - Klunzinger's Wrasse) or the local common name (*Acanthurus sohal* from the Arabic name of this Surgeonfish). At times a little poetic imagination is allowed to sneak in as in the naming of the pretty orange-yellow Blenny, *Ecsenius midas.*

Related genera are grouped together in families. In the animal kingdom the names of families always end with - **idae.** eg. Pomacanthidae (Angelfish) or Labridae (Wrasses). Members of a family share a number of characteristics of appearance, anatomy or behaviour but they are not as obviously similar as members of the same genus. There is no mistaking, even upon casual observation, the family relationship amongst the Parrotfishes. The Wrasses are much more diverse in appearance but have similarities such as tooth structure and methods of reproduction. The Wrasse family (Labridae) is a very large one, containing over 500 species worldwide. An example of a very small family is the Fistulariidae (Cornetfish) which has only 4 species.

Common names are much more confusing and vary throughout the world. Some common names are a direct translation of the scientific names. This is often true of fish whose scientific name stems from an obvious physical feature (e.g.

Eightline Wrasse). Some are named after their discoverer (eg. Weber's Chromis). Many common names are derived from names used by the local population of the area where the fish is found (e.g. Sohal). Common names can be very puzzling e.g. in the case of 'hogfish' especially when applied to the very graceful looking Lyretail.

Dr. John Randall's work (Red Sea Reef Fishes) is still the only recent authoritative systematic investigation of Red Sea fishes and his terminology has been generally followed in both scientific and common names in this book. It should be noted, however, that since publication of his work, Randall has changed, (and endorsed changes suggested by others), the scientific names of some fishes - an example being the genus *Adioryx* which is now confirmed as *Sargocentron* (Squirrelfishes). There have been a number of changes, and the authors have included as many as are known to them.

Ecological note

It is of constant amazement to us that despite the increasing abuse of the Red Sea and its coastline, the Red Sea does appear to have considerable resilience to the destructive efforts of man. It may be that the environment is far more stable than it would appear - its beauty may lead us mistakenly to deduce that it is fragile.

During our ten years of snorkelling and diving in and along the Saudi Arabian coastline we have noticed a marked deterioration in the quality of water and cleanliness of the area between fringing reef and shoreline. The effect has been a noticeable reduction in the number of different species of fishes seen in these areas, but the greatest effect seems to have been on the population of molluscs. Areas which were once full of a variety of molluscs, particularly Cowries, are now empty of them. Many areas along the coastline are now largely devoid of adult Butterflyfishes, their place being taken by large schools of algae-grazing fish such as Parrotfishes and Surgeonfishes, which can still find suitable food.

The shallow lagoon areas between reef and shore along the Jeddah coastline are nurseries for many young fish. The prevailing wind is onshore, and there is no doubt that fertilised eggs of fishes spawning near the fringing reef are carried by the surface current to the lagoons where they hatch.

It is clearly of great importance that these areas be kept clean and unpolluted - perhaps of even greater importance is to allow the free flow of water within these areas. Construction of long piers, causeways and straightforward landfill out to the fringing reef are contributing significantly to the degeneration of the coastline marine life.

One answer to the question of why the Red Sea should be so resilient to man's encroachment may be that because the fringing reef is continuous along the whole length of the Sea, species can migrate along it. Areas which have been overfished, typically by spearfishermen taking for instance the larger Groupers, will eventually be repopulated by migration along the reef. This, however, would not be the case for the outer reefs which are clearly more vulnerable to overfishing, and species of fish are less easily replaced.

Marine biologists suggest that the survival of reefs is dependent upon the balanced interrelationships of the coral, algae, the fish that feed on and farm the algae, and finally the fish that predate on the resident fauna. The relationships form a survival 'ring', which can be broken by an imbalance in population of one of these elements.

The availability and use of spearguns should be properly regulated. As a sport, spearfishing requires skill and fitness and can be an exhilarating pastime. When however, SCUBA gear and spearfishing are combined it becomes sheer murder, requiring neither skill nor courage. It is perhaps a sign of our times that technology, by being readily available, has changed our perception of man's hunter instinct from a noble and challenging characteristic to one of general abhorrence. Oddly, this abhorrence does not occur with line fishing.

The apparent absence of sharks along the Jeddah coastline (and perhaps in large sections of the Red Sea) has become very noticeable. It is said that the easily caught shark is heavily overfished simply to satisfy the Far Eastern hunger for sharks fin soup. What effect the deplenishment of the shark stock will have on the marine environment is yet to be seen. The sharks are at the top of the food chain, so that reducing their numbers will surely have a significant effect on the balance of populations of those species below them.

The governments of the countries bordering the Red Sea are beginning to realise that conserving the rich variety of marine life is an investment for the future. A shark can be killed and its fin sold only once - the same shark can be 'sold' to visiting divers a countless number of times.

A note on safety

The Red Sea has its dangers. Everyone diving or otherwise entering the water should be aware of the dangers before they enter. We would suggest that 'Red Sea Safety", by Peter Vine, be essential reading for everyone. The prime rules are do not touch anything, and always wear protective footwear!

The above book covers all that the amateur diver or swimmer should be aware of so the subject will not be discussed in detail here.

There is one animal about which there is some doubt - the sea snake. We have met a number of experienced divers who say that they have seen snakes in the Red Sea. It is now generally accepted that sea snakes are not present in the Red Sea. Free swimming black/white banded eels are found in shallow water and in shallow areas amongst live coral. They have the appearance of banded snakes, but when studied will be seen to have fins! There is a family of snake-eels (Ophichthyidae), of which three are reported to inhabit the Red Sea (ref. R H Carcasson); they can bite, but are not poisonous. The 'banded sea snake' that divers claim to have seen is most probably *Myrichthys colubrinus*, a Snake Eel.

To my mind, one of the most threatening of the commonly seen fishes is the Titan Triggerfish - it is unpredictable and is well avoided if there is any doubt about its mannerism; it has very large teeth, and will bite.

Surprisingly, Barracudas are recognised as fearsome looking, but few people consider them a threat. On the whole they are not dangerous (although large solitary individuals can be very curious and often follow divers very closely, which can be unnerving) but swimmers should not allow school Barracuda to surround them. We have known of several cases of people wading in the shallows off Port Sudan being attacked by small Barracuda. On one occasion the victim died from his wounds.

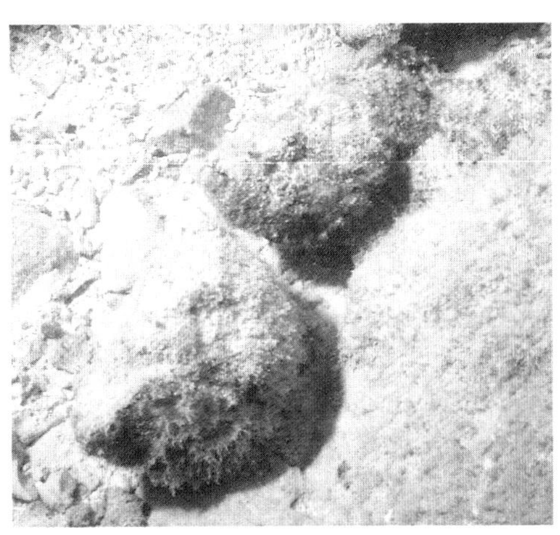

Spot the Stonefish!

One of the most misunderstood family of marine fishes is the Moray Eel family. Many people appear to subconsciously associate eels with snakes - morays are indeed, fishes - they have fins, which they use, like other fishes, to swim. They do not slide on the bottom, nor do they have poisonous fangs! However, the Moray's appearance, and its normal habit of opening and closing its mouth to induce a flow of water through it, will usually cause a sense of unease in a diver. The action of 'breathing' water presents the observer with a view of an impressive array of teeth, which are inward pointing, and clearly show that once something is in the Moray's mouth, it is unlikely to come out!

A Moray is not aggressive, and will quickly swim for cover if a diver approaches it whilst it is free swimming. However, once in its lair, like any other animal, it will defend itself if provoked. We personally do not feel any inclination to stroke these creatures, and do not recommend anyone else do so. Also, to avoid any misunderstanding, We suggest that no-one should put his hand in a hole in the reef, unless he is absolutely sure that it is not the home of a Moray Eel! Dr. John Randall, in one of his most recent publications, mentions that he has been bitten nine times whilst diving, mostly as a result of placing his hand in the wrong spot. Photographers should be especially careful - we were once obliged rudely to push a diver photographer, who being intent on photographing a small fish, was slowly descending onto a very large Moray in its lair.

When diving or swimming in the sea, it is as well to take serious notice of signs of aggression in large fishes, and not to ignore them. Fish will invariably clearly indicate their intentions before an assault. Although sharks are not often seen along the coast of the mid coastal area of Saudi Arabia, when they are seen they present a minimal threat - if they were to threaten it would be quite obvious what their intentions were!

Whilst on the subject of sharks, there is a commonly held belief that sharks will not be present with Dolphins in the same immediate vicinity. This is a myth probably engendered by our affection for the Dolphin, and its reported assaults on sharks. The author can personally testify to the inaccuracy of this belief, after an incident when he entered very deep water, alone, with mask and camera (no fins), to photograph a pod of large Dolphins relaxing alongside the boat. There were three Dolphins lazily swimming across my field of view, approximately 12m from me - they watched me, stationary in the water, camera at the ready, then suddenly turned and came directly towards me in tight formation. I waited for that photo shot of a lifetime. An instinct made me look 30 degrees to my right, which revealed to my horror, a large shark, pectoral fins pointing sharply downward, moving towards me at about half the distance of the Dolphins! The shark was one of the pelagic species, not one to ignore. Feeling extremely vulnerable I struggled the 2m back to the safety of the boat, as quickly as I could, strongly conscious of my lack of fins.

After this incident, I reflected on the action of the Dolphins - was the reason for turning towards me, in very tight formation, to warn off the shark ? It may be presumptious to deduce that they were protecting me, but the incident has certainly not diminished my respect for these wonderful creatures.

Comments for the aspiring fish photographer

Imagine being somewhere between Earth and Mars taking photographs of a passing asteroid. Every movement you make is amplified, all reactions are over-reactions, the subject is moving at thousands of kilometres per minute, and all the while you are conscious of those unfriendly Martians about to attack you from behind.

In essence, fish photography presents the same problems, without perhaps the drama. Added to these circumstantial problems of photography is the guilt you feel in breaking many of the basic rules conceived to make SCUBA diving a safe occupation. Fish do not suffer decompression problems so can swim rapidly upwards or downwards, sufficiently to make any following photographer dizzy. As for holding one's breath when taking the photograph, the less said the better!

The underwater photographer is faced with problems of his own, weightless, movement caused by his breathing (vertical movement) and the inevitable water current (horizontal movement). The subject is invariably a small, quick little creature, quite uncooperative (fish will seldom present a side view), ready to dart into cover at the sound of the diver exhaling or the sight of his bubbles.

To make the task finally impossible, a good camera and housing requires two hands to operate it, so holding on to a rock or piece of dead coral is out of the question!

Fish seldom present a side view

So much for the problems at the 'sharp end'. Consider now the aspects of providing support needed to get to the point of pressing the camera trigger.

The first requirement is a healthy bank account. The first camera purchased will be very expensive - the next will be more so, and so on. The authors, as amateurs, have six cameras which they use underwater. As new cameras are purchased, so are the strobes and flash units. Replacement parts are heavily overpriced for what they are, and good labour scarce and costly.

As well as high capital start-up costs, continuing expenditure on film and processing can be a constant heavy drain on financial resources. In terms of productivity, the average amateur may expect one acceptable photograph out of ten taken.

The second basic requirement is dedication. There are always disappointments - forgot to load film in the camera, the shark is out of focus, horror of horrors the camera has flooded! There have been many would-be underwater photographers who have purchased cameras and who have used them no more than half a dozen times. The first results underwater are guaranteed to be disappointing, simply because the physical difficulties of the environment are usually underestimated.

To enjoy underwater photography, good care of cameras, strobes and housings is of paramount importance. They all need thorough inspection and cleaning before and after use. The components of the camera system should always be taken apart when not in use, be it even for one day. The author spends more time cleaning, repairing and servicing camera systems than he spends in the water!

For those aspiring photographers setting out from Europe to an exotic underwater world my advice would be to have equipment competently serviced (better to do it oneself, confidence permitting) before departure. It is an unfortunate fact of life that exotic places often lack technical facilities and expertise, let alone spare parts. The keen photographer must be prepared to repair (or rescue!) his equipment in very difficult conditions, such as on a rocking boat in a poorly lit cabin whilst perspiring profusely in a humid air temperature of 45 degrees!

It is a characteristic of our times that we rely more and more on sophisticated technology to give us more scope and better quality in the products of our pursuits. This characteristic is particularly true in photography. There is now a broad range of camera systems and accessories that can be used underwater, with or without a housing. The price of these systems appears to be related to the amount of electronics incorporated into them. It is perhaps ironic that I find myself using today the same basic system that I built myself in 1965! In that year I built a housing using sections of building girders welded together, with linkages and seals made from cast off telegraph communications equipment. In it I placed a $15 camera, with adjustable focus and aperture. Basically this was all I needed in the bright clear waters along the Sudanese coast. I now use an aluminium housing with either an Olympus OM1, which has no electronic components or an OM40 which has been stripped of all electronics. We do, of course, use electronic flash and a film winder.

The advances in camera design have been geared to land usage, not the inhospitable depths of the sea, where a smart camera can easily be fooled by water conditions, distance measurement and colours. The circumstances in the water are such that divers wear masks, and no amount of flashing LEDs exposure indicators and warning lights in the viewfinder can help a shortsighted underwater photographer. What is actually needed is, simply, an extra large viewfinder.

Some electronic features can be useful (such as TTL strobe synchonisation) but when cameras employ electronic means to perform mechanical actions they become useless should salt water enter them. It takes a strong heart to pour fresh water into the bowels of a flooded camera full of electronic wizardry - with a mechanically operated camera however, with adequate care, problems will not arise and the camera can be used the next day. We still use a Nikonos III that has been flooded many times over its 20 year life.

Whilst the author has elected to photograph the reef fishes, others may be more interested in the photography of invertebrates, corals and reef formations. As static subjects some of the limitations mentioned above would not apply, and good results may be more forthcoming. Macro photography is now available to the pleasure diver equipped with suitable housing, strobe and lens. This form of photography can be very rewarding, and is probably the least difficult of the underwater options. Close-ups of small creatures, coral polyps and the like can look very professional and impressive.

For a real challenge the underwater photographer should look no further than the small reef fishes - good results, however infrequent, are earnt by perseverance under very adverse conditions, a well maintained camera system and of course a fair amount of luck.

General sensory characteristics of fishes

Fishes are believed to be the oldest group of vertebrates (animals with backbones) and it is thought that all other vertebrates evolved from them.

There are more than 20,000 species of fish known - about 40% of all living vertebrate species.

External anatomy of fishes

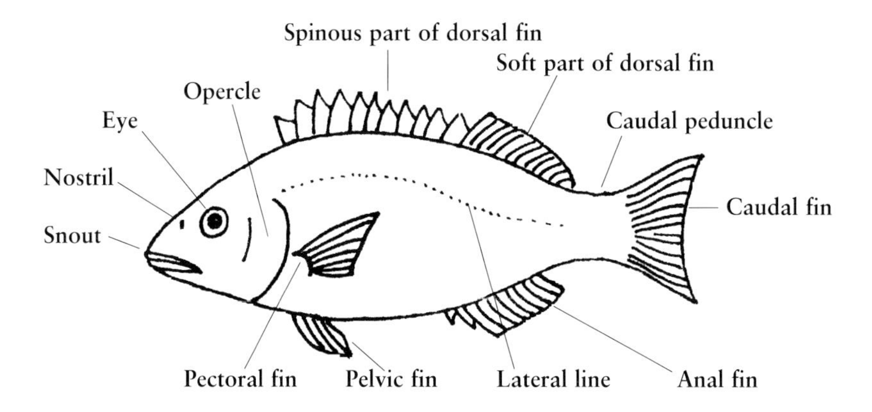

Fishes 'breathe' by means of their gills. Water is sucked in through the mouth - then with the mouth closed the water is forced over the gills and out through the opening of the operculum. As the water passes over the feathery surface of the gill filaments oxygen is taken out of it and waste carbon dioxide is passed into it.

Fishes have a well-developed nervous system. Of the senses, that of smell is especially keen, so that very small concentrations of substances can be detected. Sharks, as an example, can detect minute quantities of blood in the water, and salmon are thought to find their home waters guided by their sense of smell.

The lateral line (clearly visible in most fishes as a curved line from operculum to caudal peduncle) detects vibrations and pressure changes in the water. In some fishes changes of water temperature are also detected. Research scientists have recently concluded that the lateral line also assists shoaling fishes to synchronise their movement. This is achieved by subtle changes in light refraction, and hence colour, and thus serves as an optical communication system.

Fishes are the only animals that can generate and discharge electricity - Electric Eels, Rays and Catfishes produce a current strong enough to stun prey.

Most fishes have well developed vision. Focusing is, however, limited and is usually achieved by moving the lens towards, or away from the retina. Fishes living in shallow water are thought to have limited colour vision.

Mimicry amongst Red Sea reef fishes

The Red Sea is universally regarded as a showplace of the marine world. The beauty of its coral and animal inhabitants draws visitors from all parts of the world.

But beauty is only skin deep - what lies beneath the skin is a fish eat fish world and an animal kingdom struggling for survival against assault and predation. The huge schools of marauding Jacks and Tunas, the wolves of the sea, are ever present, keeping the little fishes of the reef constantly on the alert. However, there is also danger from within the shoaling fishes crowding the reefs, in the form of deceitful and often malevolent mimic fishes.

It is only perhaps after many dives in the Red Sea that we begin to look beyond the beauty of it all to what is really happening in the cause of survival. Have divers ever wondered why a large fish, apparently being cleaned of parasites by a cleaner fish should suddenly jerk violently in anger and chase away its cleaner? The chances are that a cleaner mimic had just taken a bite of its flesh!

Mimicry is quite a common phenomenon amongst Red Sea fishes. Since there are over 1,000 species of fishes in the Red Sea that can be loosely called reef fishes, it should not be surprising that one species may be similar in appearance to another, unrelated, species. In a number of cases the resemblance between two species can be such that it is extremely difficult to tell them apart.

From the point of view of physical appearance there are two broad categories into which mimic fishes will fit - in the first, and largest category the mimic is born as a close colour and form copy of another species, and has an acquired knowledge of how to exploit its similarity (the Natural Mimic). The second category includes those fishes that are able to adapt their colour and colour pattern to match another species, at will (the Adaptive Mimic).

The type of mimicry can be either Aggressive or Defensive. Aggressive mimicry can be described as using a natural or adaptive disguise to approach potential prey, whilst Defensive mimicry is a disguise to avoid being the prey.

The Natural Mimics form the largest group of imitators. Divers and snorkellers will be familiar with the Cleaner Wrasse *(Labroides dimidiatus)*, and may have spent many minutes watching this little fish at a cleaning station in the reef. Other fishes will allow the Cleaner Wrasse access to all parts of the body for cleaning purposes - the Cleaner Wrasse is therefore an ideal model for scale and flesh eating species which can, through their appearance, pretend to be the useful Cleaner.

The Cleaner Wrasse has two adult mimics, one of which, the Mimic Blenny *(Aspidontus taeniatus tractus)* is a natural mimic and is an almost exact copy of the Cleaner, even as a juvenile. To identify the mimic, the diver should study not the appearance, but the behaviour of this fish - physically they are different, the most significant differences being the location of the mouth and the shape of the tail fin, but these differences are usually difficult to see. When a true Cleaner approaches a potential host, it will, if unsure of its reception, perform a 'dance' before the host to be - this appears to be a signal, recognised by larger fishes. The mimics have not yet learnt this trick. This same 'dance' routine incidently will be observed in very small fishes of various species, which the author assumes helps to protect them.

The second Cleaner Wrasse mimic is an adaptive mimic, the Blue Striped Blenny *(Plagiotremis rhinorhyncus)*. This Blenny has two colour forms, one being a dark yellow body with blue stripes and the other being a black body with blue stripes. In its Black/Blue form it is a passable copy of the Cleaner, which enables it to approach target fishes and quickly bite off a scale or piece of flesh.

Many juvenile Wrasses are cleaners - however two species do bear a remarkable resemblance to the juvenile Cleaner, and this resemblance is used to full advantage; these two species are the Chiseltooth *(Pseudodax moluccanus)* and the Fourline *(Larabicus quadrilineatus)* Wrasses; the Fourline continues to clean until it is almost mature.

The Blenny family of fishes provides a number of other examples of mimicry. The plankton eating Midas Blenny *(Ecsenius midas)*, a natural mimic, will be found in shoals of Anthias *(Pseudanthias squamipinnis)*, where it gains the protection of numbers. The observer must look very hard to spot this Blenny in a group of gold/red Anthias - its home is a hole in the reef, and it will dart into cover if frightened.

The Blackline Blenny *(Meiacanthus nigrolineatus)* serves as the model for two other Blennies. The Blackline belongs to the fangtooth group of Blennies and is respected by other fish since it is able to produce a venom through grooves in its teeth when defending itself.

The Red Sea Mimic Blenny *(Ecsenius gravieri)* is an almost perfect copy of the Blackline, despite being a member of the harmless Combtooth Blenny group, whose members are characterised by their blunt heads and wide mouths.

A less perfect mimic of the Blackline is Townsend's Blenny *(Plagiotremis townsendi)* - the Red Sea form of this fish (an aggressive fangtooth Blenny) is smaller and more colourful than the model, but sufficiently similar it seems, to effectively masquerade as the potentially harmful Blackline.

Predator species of fishes have learnt to respect, and avoid, species which are distasteful or venomous. Pufferfishes are well known as toxic, and are therefore most suitable models for mimics. Their shape is unusual so that few other species are able convincingly to masquerade as a Pufferfish. There is, however, a species of Filefish, *Paraluteres arqat,* (arqat in arabic means 'second coat') which mimics the common Sharp-nosed Pufferfish *Canthigaster margaritata*. The Filefish will seldom raise it's dorsal trigger thereby maintaining it's disguise. To identify the mimic, the observer should note the greater number of dorsal rays.

Whilst Pufferfishes may be difficult for other fishes to mimic, it may come as a surprise that the Longfin Comet *(Calloplesiops altivelis)* pretends to be a Moray eel! The Comet is nocturnal, usually seen at dusk - in this poor light, if the Comet feels threatened, it will partially enter a dark hole or crevice leaving its tail end facing the threat. In this position it can easily be mistaken for a Moray Eel.

An interesting case of mimicry, common but perhaps not often noticed, is that of the Twinspot Snapper *(Lutjanus bohar)* juvenile mimicking Arabian Chromis *(Chromis flaxavilla)*. These Chromis are one of the largest of shoaling Chromis fishes. Often the Snapper, almost identical in appearance except for two white spots on its body, will be seen amongst the harmless Chromis, waiting for an opportunity to seize a small unsuspecting fish.

Adaptive mimics are not as common as natural mimics. Although many fish species are able to change their colour and pattern (particularly at night) not many change for the purpose of gaining feeding advantage through mimicry. There are some apparent cases of mimicry, as demonstrated by the female Slingjaw Wrasse *(Epibulus insidiator)* and the harmless Sulphur Damselfish *(Pomacentrus sulfureus)* - the yellow female Slingjaw will often be seen near the Damselfish, but whether this is a deliberate deception or simply coincidence is conjecture. The mature Slingjaw female is coloured primarily grey, and younger examples appear to be usually yellow - it is not known whether the Slingjaw is able to change its colour at will. As a sub-adult it is coloured a deep brown.

The most common example of adaptive (and very obvious) mimicry is that of the Mental Wrasse *(Oxycheilinus mentalis)* and Goatfish. An observer can clearly witness the development of the lateral stripe in the Wrasse as it approaches a group of Goatfish feeding over the sand. Many Wrasses are freeloaders, but this species has developed its technique to a fine art.

Jacks are voracious predators and will often join other species in the hunt for food. A common case of mimicry amongst Trevallys is that of the association of the Bluefin Trevally *(Caranx melampygus)* with large mature Yellowsaddle Goatfishes *(Parupeneus cyclostomus)*. This particular Goatfish will feed on small fishes (the preferred diet of the Trevally) which is an unusual characteristic of this species amongst the Goatfish family.

The examples above are samples of mimicry of other fishes (interspecific) - cases of mimicry do arise of fish pretending to be unpalatable inanimate material. Such pretence is of course only suitable for small, juvenile species which typically imitate the movement of waste material in the water, such as dead leaves or detritus. Two examples of this behaviour spring to mind - firstly, the juvenile Rockmover Wrasse *(Novaculichthys taeniourus)*, and secondly the juvenile Circular Spadefish *(Platax orbicularis)*.

There may be many more examples of mimicry amongst Red Sea fishes waiting to be uncovered - it takes patience and an interest in the peculiar to spot them. We would urge all divers who visit the Red Sea to, firstly, satisfy themselves with the beauty of the Sea and then start looking at the interesting relationships that exist amongst the reef fish community. There is no point to wasting precious air in covering the greatest distance - just relax and enjoy the show!

Family descriptions

Rays

It would be incorrect to classify all Rays as reef fishes, although indeed they are all seen around and in the reef areas. They are included since two species are commonly seen in the coral environment - these are the Blue Spotted Stingray and the Electric Ray. Other larger Rays will only usually be seen in deep, open water.

Rays belong to the cartilaginous group of fishes which includes Sharks and Skates. The largest family of Rays is the Stingray (Dasyatidae) family which is represented in the Red Sea by eight species. These are smooth skinned, disc shaped, mollusc eating creatures equipped with a usually long tail which is armed with one or two poisonous spines on the top. They are dangerous if frightened, or when handled carelessly.

The very common Blue Spotted Ray (sometimes known as the Lagoon Ray) is seen at all depths within amateur diving limits, and snorkellers will also see them in the shallows. Buff coloured, with bright blue spots on top of its disc, it is unmistakeable.

Other species of Stingray will be less frequently encountered, although the Longtailed (or Coachwhip Ray) is fairly common in deeper water. This Ray can be quickly recognised by its incredibly long tail, which is nearly twice its body length. When free swimming along the reef face, it appears a sandy colour with dark spots - on the bottom in the sand it adopts a much darker brown colour.

The Cowtail Stingray is similar to the Longtailed - it appears black and its tail has a distinctly broader base than the Longtailed.

Electric Rays may be quite common in the Red Sea, but they are not often observed. They are bottom-dwelling fishes, often buried in sand. However an Electric Ray will occasionally be seen 'fanning' it's way along a reef (its swimming action is suggestive of an oversize nudibranch), looking for a sandy hole to hide in. Although only two species are recorded as present in the Red Sea, the photograph shows a third that has not been reported, except by Debelius. It is brown/yellow in colour, marked by dark blotches, and is recognisable by its round disc, short tail supporting two overlarge dorsal fins.

The defence equipment of Electric Rays includes two electrodes, each side of the head, between head and pectoral wing. It should be handled with care, since it produces a considerable voltage. Once its battery has been discharged however, it may take hours to recharge.

The Red Sea is blessed with two spectacularly graceful pelagic Rays, in the Myliobatidae and Mobulidae families. These are the Eagle Ray and the Giant Manta, both of which will be seen by divers and snorkellers at a short distance from the fringing reef. Both species (like Dolphins) appear to enjoy an occasional leap out of the water (their re-entry is less graceful than that of the Dolphin!). Manta Rays will sometimes be seen in groups swimming just above the bottom, feeding on planktonic material.

Eagle Rays are dark with white spots on the top of their wings, white underneath. They have a distinctly large head, bearing large eyes.

Longtailed Stingray *Himantura uarnak*

Size: to 120cm (body length)

Found in deeper water over sandy bottoms, where it will often be covered in sand.

Forsskål, 1775

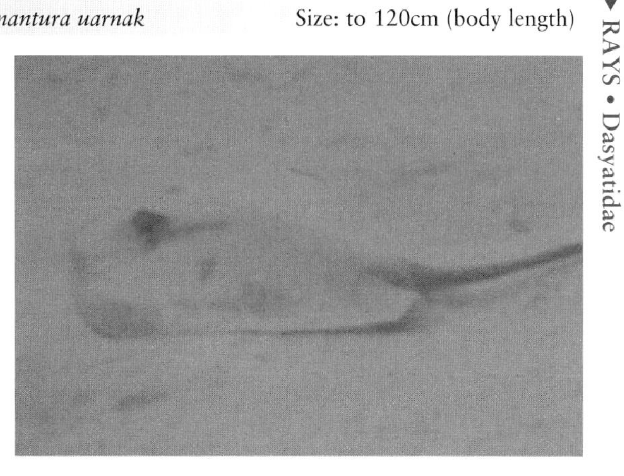

Bluespotted Stingray *Taeniura lymma*

Size: to 100cm (body length)

Very common, in shallows and on the first shelf. Prefers position under coral overhangs.

Forsskål, 1775

Electric Ray *Torpedo sp.*

Size: to at least 35cm

Occasionally seen free swimming near the reef, but usually hidden by day partially buried in sand.

Possibly *Torpedo fuscomaculata*

The Giant Manta is recognised by its uniform buff colour, and its distinctive pair of fins (lobes) in front of its mouth. When approached, a Manta Ray may suddenly 'crash dive' to deeper water - when this happens, snorkellers should be prepared to serve as temporary host to a discarded sucker fish!

Sting Rays (Dasyatidae)

Himantura	*uarnak*
Hypolophus	*sephen*
Taeniura	*lymma*
Taeniura	*melanospilos*

Eagle Rays (Myliobatidae)

Aetobatus	*narinari*

Manta Rays (Mobulidae)

Manta	*birostris*
Mobula	*thurstoni*

Electric Rays (Torpedinidae)

Torpedo	*panthera*
Torpedo	*sinuspersici*

Moray, Snake & Conger Eels

As with so many of the Red Sea fish species, authors do not agree on the number of species of Moray and Snake Eel present in the Red Sea. Likewise they do not always agree on generic classification. It appears, however, that there may be 25 species of Moray and 23 of Snake Eels in the Red Sea.

Morays are found amongst coral, debris or wrecks, whilst Snake Eels are bottom dwellers in sandy or grassy areas. The latter burrow into the sand or silt in their search for food - they are very much thinner than the heavy looking Moray. Morays and Snake Eels grow to similar lengths, although *G. flavomarginatus* (Yellow Margin Moray) is an exception in that it reputedly grows to 150cm.

A Moray Eel spends most of the daylight hours in its lair, watching the world go by, slowly opening and closing its mouth (not an aggressive habit but a necessary one to create continuous water flow through its mouth). Although they are dangerous (one look at its sharp, inward pointing teeth is a sufficient indication that it should be treated with respect), immensely strong, and aggressive in appearance, they are safe to approach, albeit very slowly and carefully.

Morays have a highly developed sense of smell - this is a common attribute amongst fishes, but is understood to be exceptional in the case of Morays. At night Morays will leave their lairs to search for food, which includes Octopus as well its usual diet of small fishes, and no doubt they find their prey using their highly developed olefactory organs.

Large, older Morays will usually be solitary: those of the smaller species very often share their lairs with others of the same species.

Snowflake Moray *Echidna nebulosa*

Size: to 75cm

A shallow water species, active at night. Photo shows a Snowflake cohabiting with an unidentified companion.

Ahl, 1789

Zebra Moray *Gymnomuraena zebra*

Size: to 150cm

Secretive; not often seen by day, hunts at night.

Shaw, 1797

Yellowmargin Moray *Gymnothorax flavimarginatus*

Size: to 120cm

Fairly common at first shelf level and deeper.

Rüppell, 1830

Giant Moray *Gymnothorax javanicus*

Size: to 220cm

Largest and most commonly seen of the Morays. Various reports of individuals up to 300cm in length. Shown here being cleaned by a wrasse and three shrimps.

Bleeker, 1859

Moray *Gymnothorax sp.*

Size: 35 cm (*G. Undulatus*)

Suspected to be *G.undulatus,* but does not conform in markings. It has been found in shallow water, down to 20m. Examples observed have been found living in close proximity to other eels of the genus.

G. undulatus, Lacepède, 1803

Grey Moray *Sidera grisea*

Size: to 65 cm

Common; often in pairs or small groups. Active at night. Shown with watching Lunartail Grouper.

Lacepède 1803

Morays (Muraenidae)

Echidna	*nebulosa*
Echidna	*polyzona*
Gymnomuraena	*zebra*
Gymnothorax	*favagineus*
Gymnothorax	*flavimarginatus*
Gymnothorax	*javanicus*
Gymnothorax	*meleagris*
Gymnothorax	*nudivomer*
Gymnothorax	*rueppelli*
Gymnothorax	*undulatus*
Sidera	*grisea*

Snake Eels (Ophichthidae)

Myrichthys	*colubrinus*
Myrichthys	*maculosus*

Conger Eels (Congridae)

Conger	*cinereus*
Heteroconger	*hassi*

Eel Catfish

As an individual, the Eel Catfish is a rather repulsive looking fish - it is therefore fortunate perhaps that large adult solitary fish are not often seen; it is the large dense school of juveniles, moving as one, that is more often observed in the reef face or over sandy seagrass areas. They may often be encountered under piers and within other man made structures.

The Eel Catfish is so named for its elongate body and continuous dorsal, tail and anal fins, and of course it's four pairs of barbels resembling cat's whiskers.

Catfish are generally known as freshwater fishes, and it appears that the only known marine species to inhabit the Red Sea is the Eel Catfish.

They are easily recognised, primarily by their barbels, but also by the white (sometimes a bluish/white or yellow) longitudinal line through the dark brown upper part of the body, the lower part being white. As adults they become a uniform dark brown colour. Sub-adults in large groups will be found in dark, sand bottom caves at depths of about 20m.

The Eel Catfish has poisonous spines in its first dorsal and its pectoral fins - they can inflict a very painful wound.

Eel Catfish (Plotosidae)
Plotosus lineatus

Lizardfishes

Our young son, when he first came across a large Slender Lizardfish, took an instant dislike to this creature, the way that a child instinctively senses evil. To come across a 30cm long Lizardfish in murky water can be alarming - they lie

▼ SNAKE EELS • Ophichthidae

Banded Snake Eel *Myrichthys colubrinus*

Size: to 88cm

Seen in sheltered lagoons and seagrass beds. One report of length 97cm.

Boddaert, 1781

▼ EEL CATFISH • Plotosidae

Striped Eel Catfish *Plotosus lineatus*

Size: to 30cm

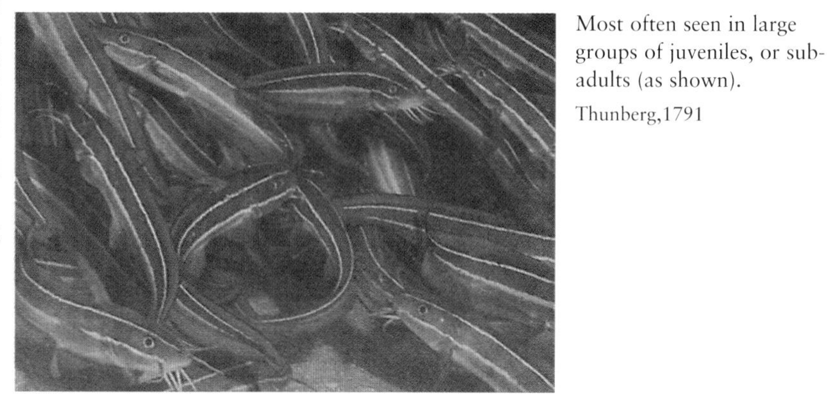

Most often seen in large groups of juveniles, or sub-adults (as shown).

Thunberg,1791

▼ LIZARDFISHES • Synodontidae

Slender Lizardfish *Saurida gracilis*

Size: to 30cm

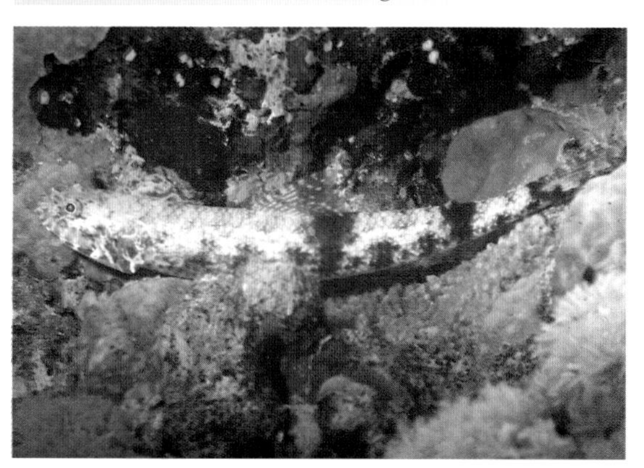

Quite common in sandy areas.

Quoy & Gaimard, 1825

Clearfin Lizardfish *Synodus dermatogenys*

Size: to 23cm

Distinguished from Common Lizardfish by black dots on top of snout.

Fowler, 1912

Common Lizardfish *Synodus variegatus*

Size: to 25cm

Common in sandy areas, often partially covered in sand, only eyes visible.

Lacepède, 1803

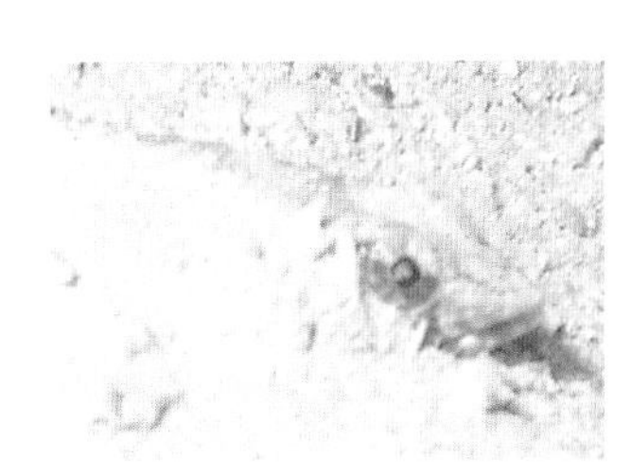

Blotcheye Soldierfish *Myripristis murdjan*

Size: to 22cm

Very common, sometimes in large groups.

Forsskål, 1775

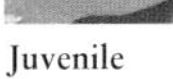

Juvenile

motionless, head raised, with their large mouths slightly open to show an immense array of fine sharp teeth, and they bear an uncanny resemblance, at least in the mind, to a waiting crocodile. They are indeed voracious predators, and will even eat their own kind, and probably their own offspring.

When they are disturbed they will shoot like a dart away from danger, often raising a cloud of sand in the process. Although usually seen lying in wait, smaller individuals have been observed free swimming amongst schools of zooplankton-eating fishes on the reef slopes.

There are 14 species of Lizardfish reported in the Red Sea, the most frequently seen being the Common Lizardfish. Others of the family will often only be seen as a pair of eyes and the tip of a snout as they lie hidden in the sandy bottom. The Common Lizardfish will often be seen in pairs - they will be observed in all areas of the reef, although perhaps more often in the silty, coral wreckage areas.

Lizardfishes (Synodontidae)

Saurida	*gracilis*
Synodus	*variegatus*
Synodus	*dermatogenys*
Synodus	*indicus*

Squirrelfishes

Squirrelfishes are very common and will always be seen by divers - snorkellers will see them if they look into dark crevices and under coral overhangs. They are most active at night when they search for larval fish and crustaceans, such as shrimps, and other small invertebrates.

Their colour is invariably some shade of red, often with silvery, yellow or brown markings. The name is derived from two characteristics - large eyes and the 'tut-tut' sound that they produce when alarmed. Some species are also known as Soldierfishes, perhaps for their red colour and the impression they give of 'standing guard' at the entrance to their shelters.

There are reportedly 15 species of Squirrelfish in the Red Sea.

The Squirrelfishes have two distinctly separate dorsal fins; the rear dorsal is almost always erect, whilst the front dorsal is usually embedded.

The larger Sabre Squirrelfish (*Sargocentron spiniferum*) appears to have a particular preference for spending the day under the shelter of Acropora coral - in so doing it is unfortunately an easy target for spearfishermen, and is often killed for its excellent tasting flesh.

The Sabre Squirrelfish has a long spine (similar to Angelfishes) on its lower cheek, which is reputed to carry venom. Fishermen in Port Sudan were very reluctant to handle these fish (although they were very fond of eating it) since they carry a number of sharp spines, particularly around the gill cover.

Spotfin Squirrelfish *Neoniphon sammara*

Size: to 25cm

Very common off the face of the reef. Previously in Genus *Flammeo*.

Forsskål, 1775

Silverspot Squirrelfish *Sargocentron caudimaculatum*

Size: to 24cm

Commonly seen at base of reef, under overhangs or in crevices.

Rüppell, 1838

Crown Squirrelfish *Sargocentron diadema*

Size: to 16cm

Usually seen in groups under overhangs and ledges during the day.

Lacepède, 1802

Squirrelfishes (Holocentridae)

Sargocentron	*caudimaculatum*	*Neoniphon*	*sammara*
Sargocentron	*diadema*	*Myripristis*	*murdjan*
Sargocentron	*ubrum*	*Myripristis*	*xanthacrus* [1]
Sargocentron	*spiniferum*		
Sargocentron	*punctatissimus*		
Sargocentron	*ittadai*		
Sargocentron	*macrosquamis*		
Sargocentron	*marisrubri* [1]		

1 Red Sea species

An unusual species in the order Beryciformes is the Flashlight Fish, *Photoblepharon palpebratum*, of the Anomalopidae family - to the authors' knowledge it has only been reported from the northern Red Sea.

It occurs in deeper water (30m) and is characterised by its ability to generate light to attract its principal food, zooplankton. The Flashlight fish is endowed with luminescent patches below its large eyes - luminescence is created by light generating symbiotic bacteria when they are fed oxygen. A black membrane covers the patch when the fish is not feeding, so the fish appears to switch the light source on and off at will.

Cornetfishes

There is no mistaking the Cornetfish. This long stick-like animal, with disproportionately large eyes will often be seen by snorkellers, usually at the edge of the fringing reef. The single species of Cornetfish in the Red Sea is one of 4 known world wide. Distantly related to the Pipefish family, it boasts a long tubular snout with which it is able to suck in and devour small fish. It characteristically "hangs" in the water, the theory being that it will drift into shoals of small fish without alarming them, and once in, will devour one of their number.

The Cornetfish is round in cross-section, has a very small single dorsal fin at the rear of its body, beyond which is a long extension ending in a tiny forked caudal fin.

They are usually found in groups, and with each fish aligned in a different direction they can make the reef edge look very untidy! As if a passing boat had discarded a load of sticks.

At night they appear to sleep, suspended in the water.

Cornetfish will sometimes be found close to the bottom of the first shelf. When near the bottom they have been seen to adopt a camouflage of dark bands - the unusual location and colour pattern may be related to mating activity, though they seem to be alone.

Cornetfishes (Fistulariidae)

Fistularia commersonii

Sabre Squirrelfish *Sargocentron spiniferum*

Size: to 45cm

Usually hiding in the reef by day, but sometimes seen under table coral.

Forsskål, 1775

Cornetfish *Fistularia commersonii*

Size: up to 150cm

Found in groups at edge of reef and above first shelf. Sometimes exhibits a pattern of wide vertical bars.

Rüppell, 1838

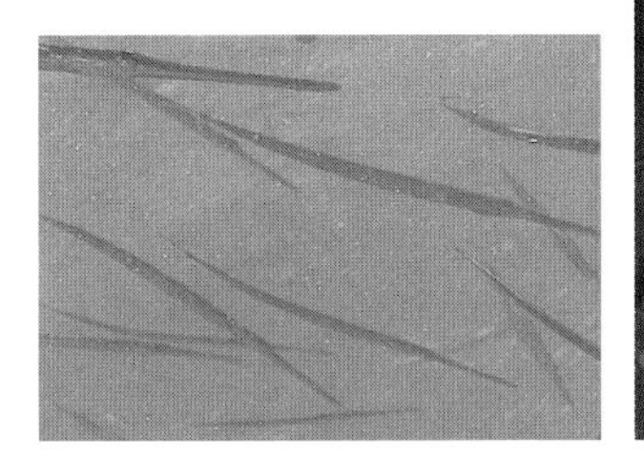

Network Pipefish *Corythoichthys flavofasciatus*

Size: to 12cm

Very common, usually in pairs, sometimes in groups.

Rüppell, 1838

Pipefishes & Seahorses

Pipefishes are well represented in the Red Sea, there being at least 33 species reported. With the single exception of the Network Pipefish, which is seen throughout the amateur diver's range, Pipefish are seldom seen. They are generally secretive and not very active by day - they will, however, be seen at night, but are slow moving, shy, and difficult to observe.

They have a delicate appearance, with their long protuding tube-like mouth and elongate body bearing the smallest of fins. They possess a single dorsal fin, with no spines, and some species have a disproportionally large tail fin, whilst others have none. They have an armoured body, being encased by bony rings.

Despite their delicate appearance, they seem to be very hardy and well able to protect themselves - I have kept a small Orangestripe Pipefish in an aquarium, cohabiting with a variety of carnivorous fish, for three years - in that time it has grown to 4cm, apparently eating minute creatures, presumably crustaceans, and showing no interest in prepared food.

Pipefishes mate by male and female curling together in a vertical plane, as the female deposits her eggs into the male's pouch. The male then carries the developing young until they are ready to face the world.

The Pipefishes are generally small (an exception is the Double-Ended Pipefish which grows to 40cm); however, there is a separate family (Solonostidae) which contains species of Ghost Pipefish which are so small and well camouflaged that they will seldom be seen by casual observers. They prefer a soft coral environment, where they adopt a colour to match the coral. They differ in their breeding habits in that the female incubates the eggs.

The Seahorses are included in the Pipefish family, but are rarely, if ever, seen in the reef environment - they prefer a seagrass environment, so will more likely to be seen in the southern Red Sea.

Syngnathidae

Seahorses

Corythoichthys *flavofasciatus*
Corythoichthys *nigripectus*[1]
Corythoichthys *schultzi*
Hippocampus *histrix*

Pipefish

Doryrhamphus *dactyliophorus*
Doryrhamphus *multiannulatus*
Doryrhamphus *excisus abbreviatus*[1]
Trachyrhamphus *bicoarctatus*

Solenostomidae

Ghost Pipefish

Solenostomus *paradoxus*
Solenostomus *cyanopterus*

1 Red Sea species

Gilded Pipefish *Corythoichthys schultzi*

Size: to 15cm

Not common. Characterised by its very long snout.

Herald, 1953

Bluestripe Pipefish *Doryrhamphus excisus abbreviatus*

Size: to 6cm

Rare; may be seen hiding amongst sea urchin spines.

Dawson, 1981

Multibar Pipefish *Doryrhamphus multiannulatus*

Size: to 18cm

Rare; may be seen at night amongst coral.
D. dactyliophorus has the same colouring but much fewer red bars. Previously in genus *Dunkerocampus*

Regan, 1903

Sea Moth

The Sea Moth (otherwise known as Dragonfish) is a very strange creature which, biologically, is not well known. There are perhaps 5-6 species worldwide, but we have found only one in the Red Sea.

Originally it was thought to be a member of the Pipefish family because it has a long tubular snout - however it clearly has a small mouth under the snout, and one school of thought was that it belonged to the Scorpionfish group - current thinking, however, is that it should be placed in its own Order. In classifying this fish therefore, I have included it in the order Pegasiformes, following Wheeler and Carcasson.

This small fish's body is entirely encased in armour, except for its tail. It has very large pectoral fins which give it the appearance of a prehistoric bird. It is indeed a very poor swimmer, and moves slowly along the bottom, occasionally taking off and 'gliding' for a short period.

It is found, albeit rarely and usually in pairs, on a sandy bottom and in shallow water (the example shown was photographed in the authors' aquarium, having been captured in shallow water).

Sea Moth (Pegasidae)
Eurypegasus draconis

Scorpionfishes

It would be a challenge to name fishes with more common names attributed to them than those of the Scorpaenidae family. Besides Scorpionfish, they are variously known as Stingfish, Chickenfish, Turkeyfish, Lionfish, Waspfish, Firefish, Dragonfish, Scorpion-cod or, it seems, any other name that suggests danger - and dangerous they are, if handled. All the members of this family (there are 90-100 species in the Indian Ocean region and 40 in the Red Sea) have poisonous spines, which can cause a very painful wound.

Since the Scorpaenidae family is so large, there is considerable variation in the characteristics and common naming of individual species. Ideally individuals of this family are best described by formal scientific names. For the purposes of 'casual' identification this book refers to the fishes of the genus *Pterois* and *Dendrochirus* as Lionfish, *Scorpaenopsis* and *Inimicus* as Scorpionfish and *Synanceia* as Stonefish.

Generally, fishes of the Scorpaenidae family have an armoured head, often with filamentous cirri, large mouth and long, well-developed spines. Many sport very large pectoral fins.

Double-ended Pipefish *Trachyrhamphus bicoarctatus*

Size: to 40cm

Found in silty or grassy areas. Example shown (about 38cm) photographed at midday, near Jeddah. When approached, rocks its head from side to side. Name derives from lack of tail fin.

Bleeker, 1857

Sea Moth *Eurypegasus draconis*

Size: to 7cm

Moves very slowly along a sandy bottom using its pelvic fins, or 'glides' above bottom. Rarely seen.

Linnaeus, 1766

Indian Walkman *Inimicus filamentosus*

Size: to 25cm

An amusing species to watch - it walks very slowly on the sand using its rear pectoral rays.

Cuvier, 1829

The most frequently encountered members of the family in the Red Sea are the Lionfishes. These are the dark red or brown, white striped, flamboyant fishes seen hiding during the daytime under ledges and in crevices in the reef. The most spectacular is the *Pterois miles*, which is the largest. When it feels threatened, it will spread its pectoral fins and adopt a head down posture, pointing its poisonous dorsal spines towards the threat - if a diver experiences this behaviour, he would be wise to retreat. This fish will sometimes collaborate with others of its kind in herding young fish prey by employing this attitude, but usually they are solitary, often seen quite immobile, waiting for a unsuspecting small fish. When it does lunge for a victim it does so with incredible speed, belying its sedentary nature. At night, these fishes will hunt in open water at the edge of the reef. Divers should beware of swimming into an individual by accident, since they appear to be deeply absorbed in their hunting activity and will not move out of the way. If a diver should shine a torch on a small bottom dwelling fish, the Lionfish will slowly approach the potential meal, and if allowed to, will swiftly devour it.

P. radiata is less willing to venture into open water during the day. It has a similar colour pattern to *P. miles,* but is usually more red than brown, and it has shorter spines and smaller fin rays. It is smaller than the *P. miles* and spends much of the daylight hours hiding under or in coral formations. Like all members of the Scorpaenidae family they prefer to wait for a meal to come to them, although at night they can be seen in the open on the bottom. Although not often noticed, they are not uncommon in the lagoon areas.

Scorpionfishes are the masters of disguise, and, (unlike the Lionfishes) can adapt their colours and colour pattern to their surrounds, so that they become extremely difficult to see. Their most noticeable characteristic is the pattern on the large pectoral fins, which often stands out against the fishes' chosen background.

One of the oddities of the Scorpionfish family is the Indian walkman. If found, it will most likely be in motion, very slowly 'walking' on the sandy seabed. It uses its rear pectoral rays to walk. When alarmed, it will spread its fins to show its magnificently coloured pectoral and tail fins, which appear much like butterfly wings.

The Shortfin Lionfish (*Dendrochirus brachypterus*) also opens out its pectorals in a similar manner to the Walkman, but its rays are not so brightly coloured, nor are they used for 'walking'.

The most notorious fish of this family of somewhat ugly fish, is the Stonefish, with its warty, filamentous surfaces; this fish can be quite invisible to the casual diver and snorkeller. It is extremely venomous, and can even cause death to the unfortunate who may tread on this fish's spines. It is fortunate perhaps that the Stonefish usually positions itself against coral rock, so the chances on treading on it are remote.

There is another group of scorpaeniform fishes that will be seen in shallow sandy areas, usually stationary under a coral overhang or beside a coral outcrop.

Lionfish *Pterois miles*

Size: to 35cm

Common, cautious by day, active at night. Base colour can be almost black, and stripes sometimes variable. *P. miles* is the Red Sea form of *P. volitans*.

Bennett, 1828

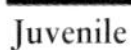

Juvenile

Clearfin Lionfish *Pterois radiata*

Size: to 20cm

Common, usually hiding by day, roaming at night. Variations in the width and pattern of stripes

Cuvier, 1829

Bearded Scorpionfish *Scorpaenopsis barbatus*

Size: to 22cm

Usually seen motionless, on coral or rubble. Spines are particularly venomous.

Rüppell, 1838

Juvenile

Devil Scorpionfish *Scorpaenopsis diabolus*

Size: to 30cm

Not very common, and difficult to see. Highly camouflaged to suit locality.

Cuvier, 1829

False Stonefish *Scorpaenopsis gibbosa*

Size: to 15cm

Not easily noticed, due to its small size and disguise.

Bloch & Schneider, 1801

Large Bearded Scorpionfish *Scorpaenopsis oxycephalus*

Size: to 35cm

Similar to *S. barbatus*, but larger.

Bleeker, 1849

Stonefish *Synanceia verrucosa*

Size: to 35cm

Most common in sandy, or rubble areas, and almost indistinguishable. The most venomous fish in the Red Sea.

Bloch & Schneider, 1801

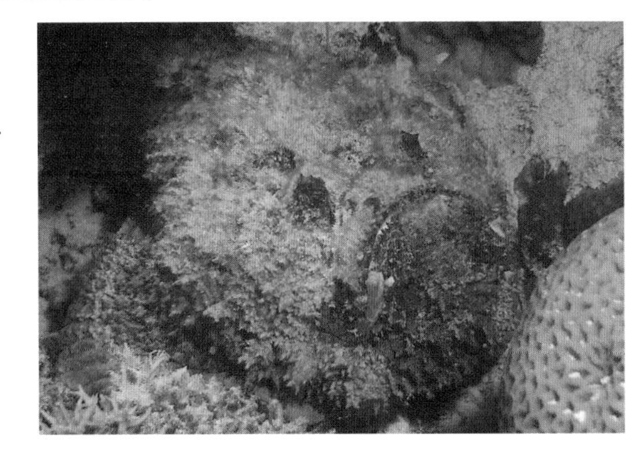

Tentacled Flathead *Papilloculiceps longiceps*

Size: to 70cm

Usually on sand, near or under reefs.

Cuvier, 1829

Indian Flathead *Platycephalus indicus*

Size: to 100cm

Found in shallow sandy areas.

Linnaeus, 1758

These are fishes of the Flathead family, which all have heads reminiscent of crocodiles - like the crocodile, they lie in wait for passing prey.

Scorpaenidae

Scorpionfish

Inimicus	*alamentosus*
Inimicus	*filamentosus*
Scorpaenopsis	*barbatus*
Scorpaenopsis	*diabolus*
Scorpaenopsis	*oxycephalus*
Scorpaenopsis	*gibbosa*

Stonefish

Synanceia	*verrucosa*

Flatheads (Platycephalidae)

Cociella	*crocodila*
Papilloculiceps	*longiceps*
Platycephalus	*indicus*

Lionfish

Dendrochirus	*brachypterus*
Pterois	*radiata*
Pterois	*miles*

Angelfishes

Angelfishes are a common sight on all reefs, slowly slipping through gaps in the coral searching for food. The shape of these sometimes large fish suggests that they were custom designed to slip through narrow crevices and gaps in the coral structures in their search. They are diurnal fishes but are usually to be found in dense aggregations of coral during the day, the larger of the species occasionally venturing out into the open water.

Juveniles are seldom seen, but when they are they look so different in their colouration and pattern that they could be mistaken for a different species from the adult. Juveniles hide in the dense corals along fringing reefs, although they are more likely to be seen in the shallow lagoon areas. The juvenile Arabian Angelfish is blue with white vertical bars, and the Yellow Bar is very similar in colours, but has a much rounder shape. The Emperor's juvenile sports a similar blue base colour, but the white bars form roughly concentric rings on the side of the fish.

Although there are some 30 species of Angelfish in the Indian Ocean region there are only 8 reported to live in the Red Sea.

Angelfishes are closely related to the Butterflyfishes - the most significant physical difference being a projection pointing to the rear on the lower cheek. This may best be observed on the Royal Angelfish which has a very pronounced blue projection against the yellow chest.

Angelfishes can be observed at any depth down to about 40m, although the author has not observed the Zebra Angelfish in less that 20m of water in the vicinity of Jeddah.

Arabian Angelfish *Arusetta asfur*

Size: to 40cm

Endemic to the Red Sea; usually solitary, but has been observed in groups of 3 or 4; difficult to approach. Previously known as *Pomacanthus asfur.*

Forsskål, 1775

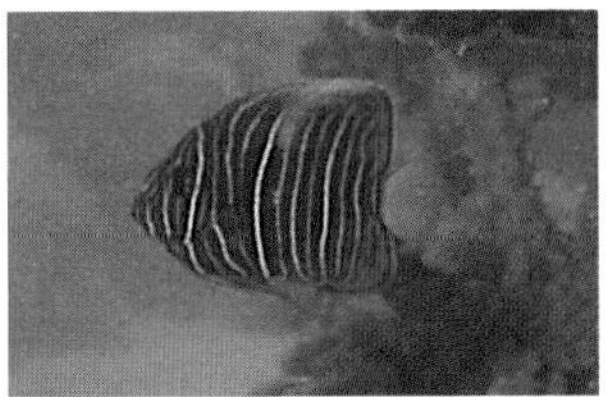

Juvenile

Multispine Angelfish *Centropyge multispinis*

Size: to 10cm

Common over shallow reef areas; very shy, darts into coral when approached

Playfair & Günther, 1866

Zebra Angelfish *Genicanthus caudovittatus*

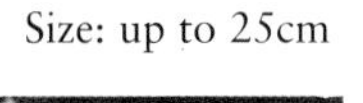

Size: up to 25cm

Female

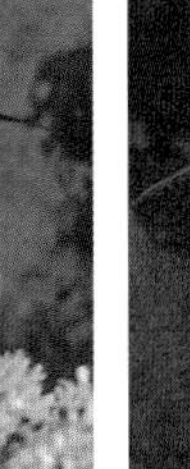

Male

Paired or in small groups; not common above 25m

Günther, 1860

Emperor Angelfish *Pomacanthus imperator*

Size: to 40cm

Usually solitary; difficult to approach. Painting of juvenile by authors' son, Francis.

Bloch, 1787

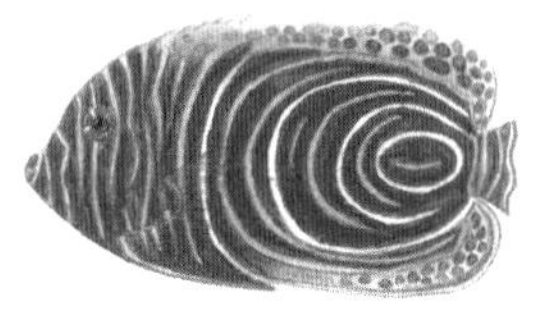

Yellowbar Angelfish *Pomacanthus maculosus*

Size: to 50cm

Adult

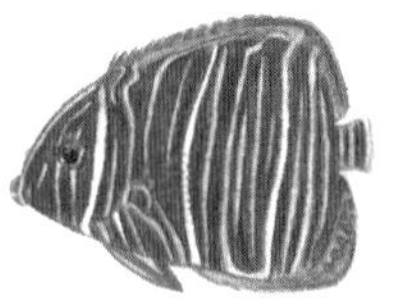

Juvenile

Sub-adult

Painting of juvenile by authors' son, Francis.

Forsskål, 1775

Royal Angelfish *Pygoplites diacanthus*

Size: to 25cm

Common down to at least 30m; solitary or in pairs; split bar patterns are common.

Boddaert, 1771

Perhaps the most noticeable of all the Angelfish along the fringing reef is the vividly coloured Royal, although the most abundant is probably the Multispine; the Multispine is much less colourful and is very cautious, and will not allow a diver to approach it.

Royal Angelfishes will often be seen with variations in the form of the vertical bars - although there are generally nine bars, some are joined to form forks, or arcs. This characteristic does not appear to be a function of age - some large specimens are marked in this way. Zebra and Emperor Angelfishes also show this characteristic.

A large Angelfish is capable of emitting a loud 'thumph' sound, which can alarm an approaching diver - they are, however, quite harmless fish which feed on algae or sponges and gorgonians. They will readily take shrimp in captivity.

Large Angelfish, particularly the Yellowbar, can be a nuisance to photographers. In areas where diving is popular, these fish become very tame, and seem to demand attention - some will follow a diver throughout his dive.

The population of some Angelfishes appears to have declined dramatically over the past few years. Most noticeable by its absence in recent years is the native Arabian Angelfish which is now not often seen - once frequently seen in shallow areas, it now seems to prefer deeper water at the 30m mark.

Angelfishes (Pomacanthidae)

Apolemichthys	*xanthotis*[1]	*Pomacanthus*	*imperator*
Arusetta	*asfur*[1]	*Pomacanthus*	*maculosus*
Centropyge	*multispinis*	*Pomacanthus*	*semicirculatus*
Genicanthus	*caudovittatus*	*Pygoplites*	*diacanthus*

1 Red Sea species

NB *Apolemichthys xanthotis* is a Red Sea variant of *Apolemichthys xanthuras,* the Indian smoke Angelfish. The authors have not, to date, found this species.

Blennies

Blennies are worldwide in distribution, with hundreds of species. In the Red Sea some 48 species have been reported. The Blenniidae family is divided into two subfamilies, commonly known as Combtooth (Salariinae) and Sabretooth (Blenniinae). The Combtooth Blennies are herbivores and the Sabretooths are carnivorous.

Combtooth Blennies are numerous in the Red Sea, but because of their small size and their tendency to lie stationary on a coral head or ledge, or in a hole, are often missed by divers and snorkellers. We have occasionally photographed a fish and found one of these creatures in the frame after processing. To find them, a selected area of reef must be carefully scanned, and every hole investigated.

Combtooth Blennies are characterised by their blunt head, with eyes at the top corners and mouth on the bottom edge - in some species the eyes seem to be forward of the mouth.

These Blennies, as a sub-family, are not confined to any specific locale. They are herbivores and are territorial, but will often share an algae garden with a Damselfish and/or a Surgeonfish. Many in the Red Sea inhabit the shallow areas amongst seagrass or silt. It is not an uncommon sight to see the Jewelled Blenny, with its tail curled ready quickly to dart away, sitting in an empty mollusc shell guarding eggs (in recent years soft drinks cans provide a modern home). When the sunlight is directly on it, the small bluish dots on its body sparkle like diamonds. Others live in coral branches, typical of which is the Short-bodied Blenny which seems to prefer the protection of fire-coral (*Millepora dichotoma*, which is not actually a coral - it is a Hydrozoan which builds a calcareous skeleton). This particular Blenny grows to be one of the largest of the family - we have observed a pair (the female with dark brown spots and the male with brilliant red spots) each of which was about 15cm in length.

Some species of Combtooth Blenny live very close to the shore line - one of the most commonly seen is the Leaping Blenny, which will perch on rocks, out of the water, and when alarmed, will leap amazing distances to safety.

Blennies of the sub-family Sabretooth are regularly encountered off the fringing reef, most notable being the Scale-eating Blenny and the various species that imitate the behaviour, and mimic the colour, of other fishes.

The imitators are of two kinds. There are two that mimic another Blenny and that are both endemic to the Red Sea. Others mimic cleaner wrasses to get close to a potential meal.

The Blackline Blenny is common along the Jeddah coastline and it serves as the model for the Red Sea Mimic Blenny and the Townsend's Blenny. The Blackline possesses a pair of sharp canine teeth on its lower jaw; they are grooved and transmit venom from a gland at the base of the teeth. Predators have learnt to respect this little fish, and keep away from it. Both the imitators mimic the colouration and the manner of the Blackline, the Red Sea Mimic being almost a replica. The Mimic can be identified by its larger eye and the black lateral line which does not meet the eye. The Townsend's Blenny is not a good colour copy of the Blackline - it is indeed a much prettier fish - but it imitates the manner and attitudes of the Blackline.

Whilst the above two mimics imitate for defensive purposes, the Bluestriped Blenny and the blue Mimic Blenny use mimicry to get closer to their next meal. The Bluestriped has only a passing resemblance to the well known Cleaner Wrasse, but sufficiently it seems to approach large fish, and, like its cousin the Scale-eater, steal a bite. The Mimic Blenny closely resembles the Cleaner Wrasse, to such a degree that the two species are extremely difficult to tell apart; the main differences are in the shape and length of its dorsal fin and the position of its mouth. The Mimic also has a reddish edge to its dorsal and anal fins. The best way to decide the identity of an individual is to study its behaviour - the Mimic

Leaping Blenny *Alticus kirkii*

Size: up to 9cm

Found on exposed rocky shores or in very shallow water. Photographed in Authors' aquarium.

Günther, 1868

Lance Blenny *Aspidontus dussumieri*

Size: up to 12cm

Only large adults exhibit the bright yellow extended two middle caudal fin rays. The Red Sea form of this species has a ventral black stripe, and a black spot on the front dorsal rays.

Cuvier & Valenciennes, 1836

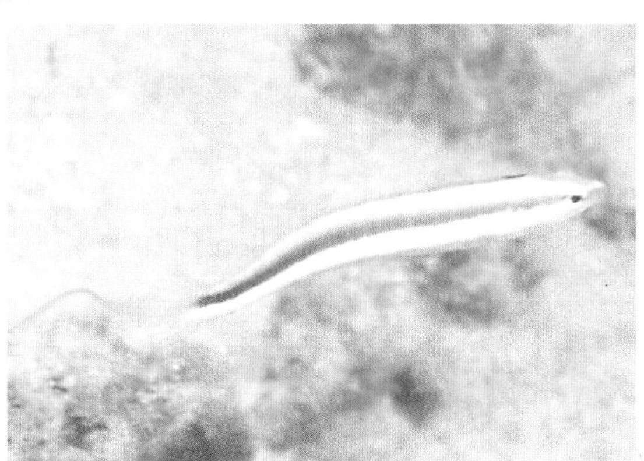

Mimic Blenny *Aspidontus taeniatus tractus*

Size: up to 11cm

A truly remarkable mimic of the Cleaner Wrasse *Labroides dimidiatus*.

Fowler, 1903

Chestnut Blenny *Cirripectes castaneus*

Size: up to 10cm

Darts quickly amongst rocks and coral on reef top. Usually all one sees is a flash of velvety brown colour; the male is shown. The female is similar, but with a honeycomb pattern on sides of body.

(Valenciennes, 1836)

Smoothfin Blenny – variant *Ecsenius albicaudatus*

Size: to 8cm

One of the two variants of *E. frontalis* (Valenciennes 1836), which is dull yellow with a bluish head. The other, *E. nigrovittatus* is found only in the southern Red Sea.

Aron's Blenny *Ecsenius aroni*

Size: up to 5.5cm

Often only the head is seen peeking out of a hole in the coral or a worm tube. Sometimes paired. Endemic to the Red Sea.

Springer, 1971

Smoothfin Blenny *Ecsenius frontalis*

Size: to 8cm

Not common - will be found on reef faces down to about 10m.

Valenciennes, 1836

Red Sea Mimic Blenny *Ecsenius gravieri*

Size: to 8cm

Mimic of venomous Blackline Blenny *(Meiacanthus nigrolineatus)*. Found only in the Red Sea and G. of Aden.

Pellegrin, 1906

Midas Blenny *Ecsenius midas*

Size: up to 13cm

Another colour form is dark blue/grey. Yellow form often seen with Anthias.

Starck, 1969

Nalolo *Ecsenius nalolo*

Size: up to 6.5cm

Common, but difficult to spot, despite being often fully exposed on coral.

Smith, 1959

Shortbodied Blenny *Exallias brevis*

Size: up to 15cm

Female has brown spots, male has bright red spots. Usually found in fire coral.

Kner, 1868

Rockskipper *Istiblennius periophthalmus*

Size: up to 15cm

Found mostly on rocky shores and under piers. A shallow water species.

Cuvier & Valeciennes, 1836

Blackline Blenny *Meiacanthus nigrolineatus*

Size: up to 9cm

Found only in the Red Sea. It has a venomous bite and is the mimic model for two non venomous Blennies. Small photo assumed to be juvenile.

Smith-Vaniz, 1969

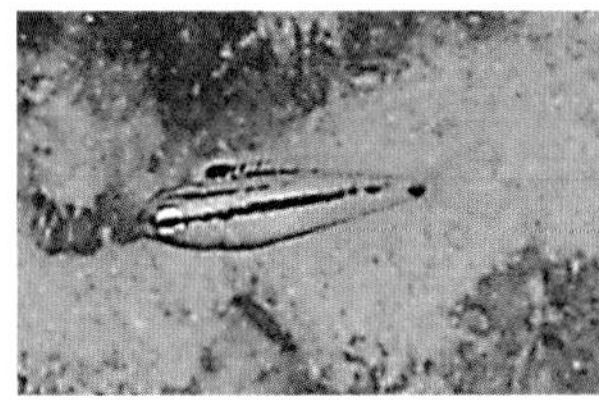

Juvenile

Bluestriped Blenny *Plagiotremus rhinorhynchos*

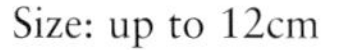

Size: up to 12cm

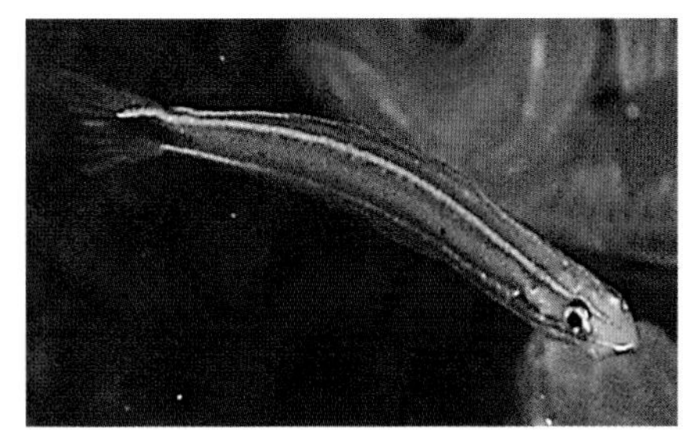

Feeds by taking bites of other fish whilst in open water. Juveniles mimic the Cleaner Wrasse which they resemble. The adult blue form is also assumed to mimic colours; although not a very close copy of the Cleaner Wrasse, the resemblance is sufficient to allow it to get close to other fish.

Bleeker, 1852

Scale-eating Blenny *Plagiotremus tapeinosoma*

Size: up to 14cm

Hovers with slow undulating motion and quickly darts in to bite other fish. It will also bite humans.

Bleeker, 1857

does not employ the Cleaner 'dance' as it approaches its target fish, and will also usually be chased away by larger fish, who have learnt to recognise it.

Another possible mimic is the Midas Blenny, which is often seen within a group of Anthias. Although its physical appearance is quite different, its colour and tail closely match the Anthias'. Why it should wish to imitate Anthias is a puzzle to the authors - perhaps it is a case of safety in numbers.

It will also be seen in the large shoals of Glassfish that hide in reef caves.

Blennies (Blenniidae)

Alticus	*kirkii*	*Ecsenius*	*albicaudatus* [1,2]
Aspidontus	*dussumieri*	*Ecsenius*	*nigrovittatus* [1,2]
Aspidontus	*taeniatus tractus*	*Exallias*	*brevis*
Atrosalarias	*fuscus*	*Istiblennius*	*edentulus*
Cirripectes	*castaneus*	*Istiblennius*	*periophthalmus*
Cirripectes	*filamentosus*	*Istiblennius*	*rivulatus* [1]
Ecsenius	*aroni* [1]	*Meiacanthus*	*nigrolineatus* [1]
Ecsenius	*frontalis* [1]	*Plagiotremus*	*rhinorhynchos*
Ecsenius	*gravieri* [1]	*Plagiotremus*	*tapeinosoma*
Ecsenius	*midas*	*Plagiotremus*	*townsendi* [1]
Ecsenius	*nalolo*	*Salarias*	*fasciatus*
Ecsenius	*dentex* [3]		

1 Red Sea species
2 Variants of *E. frontalis; E. nigrovittatus* reported only from the southern Red Sea.
3 Same as *E. nalolo* differing only in the number of incisor teeth. North Red Sea only

Butterflyfishes

No one can deny that the Butterflyfishes provide the reef environment with its most colourful and gracious fauna. Always observed in and around the reefs, Butterflyfishes move slowly and sedately between the coral outcrops gently feeding on coral polyps.

They do not appear to move far from a chosen locale, and are often seen in pairs, which suggests that they may pair for life. It certainly seems that the Masked Butterflyfish forms a lifelong bond - we have only seldom observed a solitary fish of this species.

The predominant colour of the Red Sea Butterflyfishes is yellow, and some have a dark patch around the eyes, but more commonly, they have a stripe through the eye. This latter characteristic is not common in Angelfishes, which in some ways Butterflyfishes resemble.

Butterflyfishes also have smaller mouths than Angelfishes, and these mouths protude to enable the fish to feed within coral branches. The only exception to this rule is the Exquisite Butterflyfish.

Townsend's Blenny *Plagiotremus townsendi*

Size: up to 4cm

A less perfect Red Sea mimic of the Blackline Blenny; this Red Sea form is more brightly coloured than the same species outside the Red Sea.

Regan, 1905

Jewelled Blenny *Salarias fasciatus*

Size: up to 14cm

Common in shallow water and on reef tops. Second photo shows the blenny "at home".

Bloch, 1786

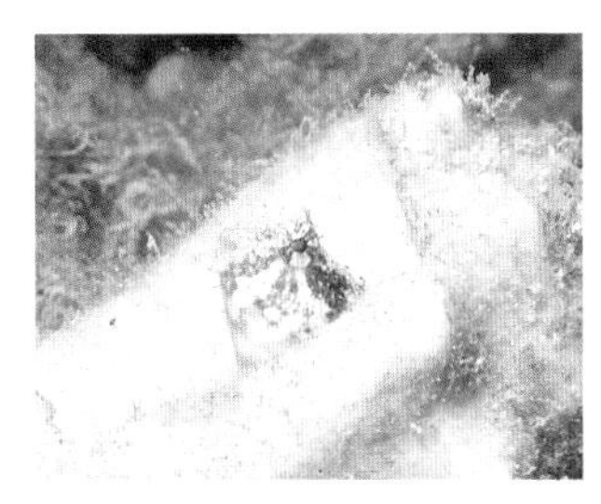

Threadfin Butterflyfish *Chaetodon auriga*

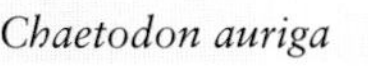

Size: to 20cm

Named for its often long trailing dorsal fin.

Forsskål, 1775

Juvenile

Exquisite Butterflyfish *Chaetodon austriacus*

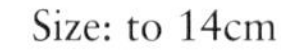
Size: to 14cm

Endemic to the Red Sea and Gulf of Aden. A related Indian Ocean species, *C. melapterus* with a black dorsal fin may be found in the southern Red Sea.

Rüppell, 1836

Striped Butterflyfish *Chaetodon fasciatus*

Size: to 22cm

Red Sea and Gulf of Aden: common, easy to approach; sometimes in small groups.

Forsskål, 1775

Orangeface Butterflyfish *Chaetodon larvatus*

Size: to 12cm

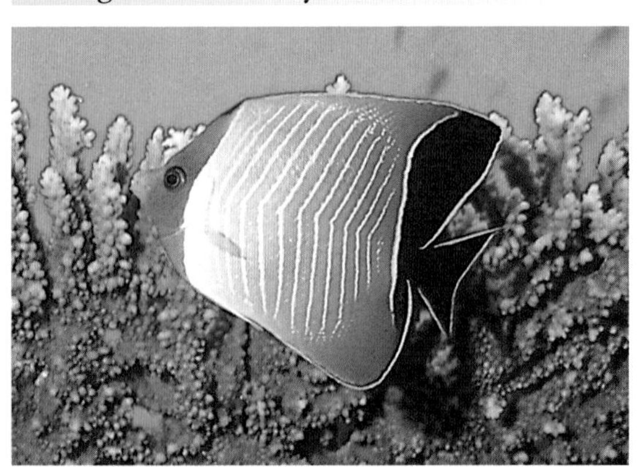

Red Sea and Gulf of Aden; usually seen busy feeding on coral; not very common. Previously placed in the Genus *Gonochaetodon*.

Cuvier, 1831

Lined Butterflyfish *Chaetodon lineolatus*

Size: to 30cm

Largest of the Butterflyfishes ; not very common; sometimes solitary.

Cuvier, 1831

Blackback Butterflyfish *Chaetodon melannotus*

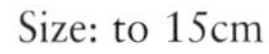

Size: to 15cm

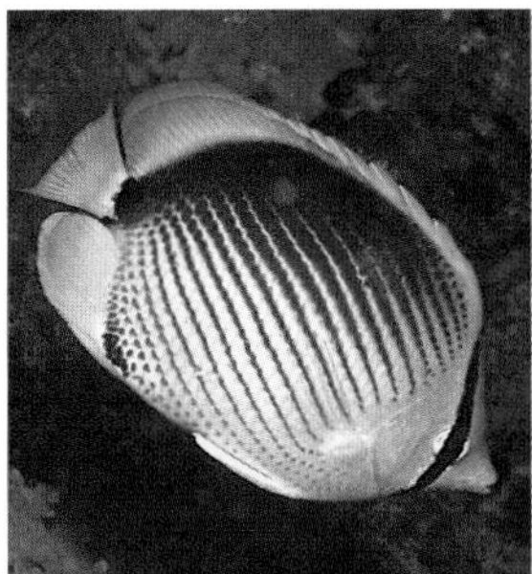

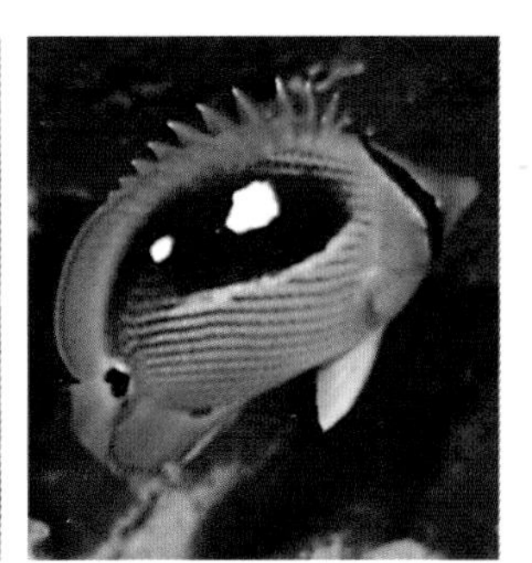

Not very common; a shy fish. Photos show juvenile, adult and night-time colours.

Bloch & Schneider, 1801

Paleface Butterflyfish *Chaetodon mesoleucos*

Size: to 14cm

Red Sea to Gulf of Aden; fairly common, especially near the fringing reef.

Forsskål, 1775

Crown Butterflyfish *Chaetodon paucifasciatus*

Size: to 14cm

Red Sea and Gulf of Aden; in pairs or small groups; quite common in deeper water.

Ahl, 1923

Masked Butterflyfish *Chaetodon semilarvatus*

Size: to 23cm

Red Sea and Gulf of Aden; arguably the most elegant of the family; always in pairs or small groups; hovers under table coral or overhangs, waiting to be photographed; quite easy to approach.

Cuvier, 1831

Red Sea Bannerfish *Heniochus intermedius*

Size: to 20cm

Red Sea and Gulf of Aden; usually paired, but smaller individuals sometimes form very large groups. Can be confused with the Pennant Butterflyfish, *H. diphreutes*.

Steindachner, 1893

Worldwide 113 species of Butterflyfishes have been recorded. It is perhaps surprising that the Red Sea only contains (as far as has been reported) 21 species of which 6 are endemic. This may suggest that Butterflyfishes are reluctant to wander far from their particular areas. It is noticeable that many juvenile Butterflyfish occur in the shallow lagoon areas around Jeddah (this suggests to the authors that their eggs float at the surface and follow the prevailing onshore wind current).

Unlike Angelfishes, juveniles are similar in colour to adults; the sexes of adults do not appear to differ in colour or pattern. Some species, however, adopt different colour patterns at night, mainly showing large white patches, containing a black smudge, on their sides.

Although most Butterflyfishes are seen in pairs, or within the general vicinity of like species, the Pennantfish and Red Sea Bannerfish will often be seen in large aggregations, apparently feeding on plankton close to the sea floor. It may be that these are young fish preparing for life and that these meetings are the start of relationships.

Although Butterflyfish are favourite aquarium fishes, we have often found that they carry minute parasites which can cause a problem in an aquarium.

Butterflyfishes (Chaetodontidae)

Chaetodon	*auriga*	*Chaetodon*	*melapterus*
Chaetodon	*austriacus*[1]	*Chaetodon*	*melannotus*
Chaetodon	*fasciatus*[1]	*Chaetodon*	*mesoleucos*[1]
Chaetodon	*guttatissimus*	*Chaetodon*	*paucifasciatus*[1]
Chaetodon	*kleinii*	*Chaetodon*	*semilarvatus*[1]
Chaetodon	*larvatus*[1]	*Forcipiger*	*flavissimus*
Chaetodon	*lineolatus*	*Heniochus*	*diphreutes*
Chaetodon	*leucopleura*[2]	*Heniochus*	*intermedius*[1]
		Megaprotodon	*trifascialis*

1 Red Sea species 2 Southern Red Sea

Cardinalfishes & Big Eyes

There are 54 species of Cardinalfish reported in the Red Sea. They are usually found hiding during the day - they are nocturnal, which accounts for their characteristically large eyes. Some species exhibit an overall shiny reddish colour, which suggests the origin of the common family name.

During the day they will be seen stationary, often in large groups, under overhangs, in crevices or amongst the spines of sea urchins - at night they become voracious predators of large zooplankton, small fishes and crustaceans. They have two distinctly separate dorsal fins, large mouths and strong tails, the latter

Chevron Butterflyfish *Megaprotodon trifascialis*

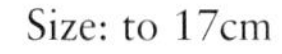

Size: to 17cm

One of the smallest of the family, often seen feeding on top of table coral. Previously classified in genus *Chaetodon*.

Quoy & Gaimard, 1825

Juvenile

Ringtail Cardinalfish *Apogon annularis*

Size: to 7cm

Endemic to the Red Sea.

Rüppell, 1829

Cook's Cardinalfish *Apogon cookii*

Size: to 10cm

Found in shallow, silty water.

Macleay, 1881

Goldstriped Cardinalfish *Apogon cyanosoma*

Size: to 7cm

Often seen hiding amongst the spines of black sea urchins, usually in shallow water.

Bleeker, 1853

Eyeshadow Cardinalfish *Apogon exostigma*

Size: to 10cm

Found in shallow, protected water often hiding amongst the spines of black sea urchin.

Jordan & Starks, 1906

Iridescent Cardinalfish *Apogon kallopterus*

Size: to 15cm

Solitary, seen in reef crevices; they will hide if approached. Older individuals appear to lose their dark band and caudal spot.

Bleeker, 1856

enabling them to move very quickly if necessary. A number of species exhibit irridescent blue markings and others are almost transparent. It would be safe to say that if a large school of tiny, shiny, motionless fish is found in a large hole in the coral, it will be a school of young Cardinalfish.

A frequently observed phenomenon is that of the larger male Cardinalfish carrying eggs (or the larvae) of its young in its mouth. The mouth becomes distended and slightly open, revealing the eggmass through an impressive array of small very sharp teeth. As keeper of the young, the male Cardinalfish must go without food for some considerable time! There has been a recent report of mouth brooding by females, but this has not been noticed by the authors.

There are estimated to be about 100 species of Cardinalfish in the Indian Ocean region, so there may be even more than 54 species in the Red Sea. Many of the different species can look remarkably similar, and require detailed examination for identification.

Big-Eyes are not related to Cardinalfishes, though in behaviour and general appearance they resemble both the Cardinalfishes and the Squirrelfishes. The only member of this family likely to be seen in the Red Sea is the Goggle-Eye. It will be found hiding during the day, in crevices in the reef face. Goggle-Eyes are a brilliant red in colour, over their entire body and fins. They can, however, assume a silver banded appearance, particularly at night when they are active. The Goggle-Eye is an unmistakable species - large eyes and a very oblique upturned mouth, and of course its brilliant, all over red colour.

It is very easily approached by divers. Interestingly, these fish appear to adopt the silver colour when approached - on one occasion the author approached a group of 7 Goggle-Eyes and those in the centre of the group turned silver, the two on the outside remained red.

Cardinalfishes (Apogonidae)

Apogon *annularis*[1]
Apogon *coccineus*
Apogon *cookii*
Apogon *cyanosoma*
Apogon *exostigma*
Apogon *fleurieu*
Apogon *fraenatus*
Apogon *kallopterus*
Apogon *leptacanthus*
Apogon *multitaeniatus*
Apogon *nigrofasciatus*
Apogon *pseudotaeniatus*
Apogon *gularis*
Apogon *taeniatus*
Apogon *taeniophorus*
Apogon *timorensis*
Archamia *fucata*
Archamia *lineolata*[1]
Cheilodipterus *bipunctatus*
Cheilodipterus *lineatus*
Cheilodipterus *macrodon*
Cheilodipterus *quinquelineatus*
Cheilodipterus *lachneri*
Cheilodipterus *arabicus*
Fowleria *variegata*

1 Red Sea species

Blackline Cardinalfish *Apogon nigrofasciatus*

Size: to 10cm

Usually solitary, hiding in reef face.

Lachner, 1953

Timor Cardinalfish *Apogon timorensis*

Size: to 9cm

Found in rocky areas or in coral.

Bleeker, 1854

Orangelined Cardinalfish *Archamia fucata*

Size: to 8cm

Found in schools at base of reef or in caves. *A. lineolata* is a related Red Sea species with fewer vertical orange lines.

Cantor, 1850

Arabian Cardinalfish *Cheilodipterus arabicus*

Size: to 15cm

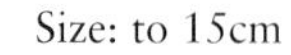

Endemic to the Red Sea; Usually seen stationary, close to the reef face.

Gmelin, 1788

Lined Cardinalfish *Cheilodipterus lineatus*

Size: to 18cm

In small groups in caves or at base of reefs.

Lacepède, 1801

Largetooth Cardinalfish *Cheilodipterus macrodon*

Size: up to 24cm

Hovers singly or in loose agg-regations at the base of reefs or at cave openings. Males can sometimes be seen with eggs or larvae in their mouth. Juveniles have a yellowish tinge.

Lacepède, 1802

Fiveline Cardinalfish *Cheilodipterus quinquelineatus*

Size: to 12cm

Often hides among the spines of black sea urchins.
C. bipartitus is very similar except for an additional black spot at the top of the caudal peduncle.

Cuvier, 1828

Goggle-eye *Priacanthus hamrur*

Size: to 35cm

Seen under ledges and in caves. Normally red but sometimes silver or with alternating wide red and silver bands.

Forsskål, 1775

Snubnose Chub *Kyphosus cinerascens*

Size: to 45cm

Found singly but usually in groups along the edge of reefs.

Forsskål, 1775

Big Eye (Priacanthidae)

Priacanthus	*hamrur*
Priacanthus	*blochii*

Chubs

Three species of Chub are found in the Red Sea, the most common being the Brassy Chub, named for its bronze appearance resulting from gold coloured lateral lines on its dark body. Chubs are rather shy and not easily approached. They usually form small schools, and are observed roving about the reef grazing on algae and vegetable matter. They will often be found around man-made structures and wreckage which provide ideal feeding grounds, with smooth surfaces and plentiful algae.

They are 'heavy' fish with a disproportionately small mouth and very large dorsal, anal and tail fins.

They are known in some areas of the world as Rudderfish, the name resulting from reports of them following closely behind ships.

Chubs (Kyphosidae)

Kyphosus	*bigibbus* [1]
Kyphosus	*cinerascens*
Kyphosus	*vaigiensis*

1 Similar in appearance to *K. vaigiensis;* differs in number of dorsal spines

Damselfishes

Damselfishes must surely be named for their appearance, not their nature!

A snorkeller swimming over the inside of the fringing reef will be aware of the fiercely aggressive Black Damselfish protecting its territory - more precisely, it is guarding a small garden of algae, which provides the fish with its main food source (this particular Damselfish often appears to share an algae garden with Surgeonfish, each protecting the patch in its own way). These, like many of the other Damsels will bite. The author experienced the unprovoked bite of a large Royal Damselfish, which left a perfectly formed square of four incisions on his arm.

Damselfishes are very common in the shallow areas, with some inhabiting the waters edge, particularly Sergeant Majors and the pretty Onespot and Threeline

Brassy Chub *Kyphosus vaigiensis*

Size: to 60cm

Found over open water off the edge of reefs. *K. bigibbus* is very similar in appearance but is not so common.

Quoy & Gaimard, 1824

Scissortail Sergeant *Abudefduf sexfasciatus*

Size: to 19cm

Very common. Often found in mixed groups with Sergeant Majors off the fringing reef.

Lacepède, 1801

Blackspot Sergeant *Abudefduf sordidus*

Size: to 22cm

Found along rocky shores; juveniles frequent very shallow inner reef areas.

Forsskål, 1775

juveniles. Most juvenile Damsels sport a false eyespot, whilst others, like the Royal Damselfish are magnificently coloured, bearing no resemblance to their adult colouration.

The Damselfish grouping (320 species worldwide, 45 reported in the Red Sea) includes Dascyllus and Chromis, most of which can be seen in shallow water. The common Banded Dascyllus is associated with stylophora coral, so is not seen below 20m - this particular Damsel lives in small colonies, and is believed to 'own' an individual private area within a coral head, which it guards closely.

Nine species of Damselfishes are reported to be found only in the Red Sea.

Chromis (alternatively known by the unflattering name 'Puller') abound along the edge of the fringing reef, and in well-lit areas of shallow reef down to 20m. A coral head may contain hundreds of these zooplankton-eating little fishes, the pretty Blue Green Chromis being very significant in large aggregations. They are very wary, and will quickly disappear into the coral branches when approached - they appear to be a favourite snack for a passing Jack. When spawning, the male Chromis adopts black edging to its fins - the act of egg laying and fertilisation appears to be a group activity.

Damselfishes are popular aquarium fishes - they are adaptable, and their nature is flamboyant. They do not, however, tolerate the intrusion of other species into their territories, and can be a problem in a crowded aquarium.

Best known perhaps of all the Damselfishes is the so called Anemone (or Clown) Fish. A diver approaching a stoichactid anemone may be greeted by an aggressive lunge by one of these fishes, warning him away. The warning will be accompanied by some loud grunting noises. In the Red Sea, the resident Anemone Fish is the Two Bar, which is endemic to the Red Sea. It differs from its cousins in other oceans (there are some 25 species known) by having two vertical bluish/white bars - the rear bar has been observed to be very faint in some older animals, which perhaps is a reversion to its Indian Ocean origins. Anemonefishes are sometimes classified in a different sub-family to the Pomacentridae (Amphiprioninae) since they have very much smaller scales - the scales are so small that they are hardly visible.

The Anemonefish is strongly associated with its anemone, with which it forms a symbiotic relationship. The exact process by which the fish becomes immune to the stings of the anemone does not appear to be fully understood. The popular theory is that the fish excretes a mucous that fools the anemone into thinking the fish is a part of itself. We have observed in the aquarium that if an anemone is replaced by a different kind, the fish will very quickly (within an hour) be quite happily nudging and brushing its new host.

A host anemone often contains a large family of fishes, presided over by one large female. Except for a single breeding male the family will remain juvenile until the female dies; the dominant juvenile will quickly grow to replace her as head of the family. This process is easily observed in an aquarium environment, as well as in the sea.

Often, the anemone hosting the Two Bar Anemonefish will simultaneously host

Sergeant Major *Abudefduf vaigiensis*

Size: to 18cm

Very common, in reef crevices and at sides of reefs; juveniles in shallows along shore line; the Indo-Pacific form is regarded as a separate species from the Atlantic *A. saxitilis.*

Quoy & Gaimard, 1824

Yellowflank Damselfish *Amblyglyphidodon flavilatus*

Size: to 9cm

Found only in the Red Sea and Gulf of Aden. Quite common along seaward reef faces, but not on top.

Allen & Randall, 1981

Juvenile

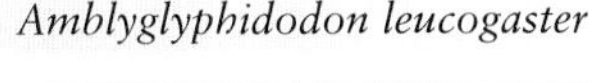

Whitebelly Damselfish *Amblyglyphidodon leucogaster*

Size: to 14cm

Very common singly or in small groups along seaward sides of reefs.

Bleeker, 1847

a group of juvenile Dominos, a Dascyllus species. These little black fishes with prominent white dots (two initially) are aptly named and appear to live quite happily sharing the anemone. A well-developed anemone inhabited by Clownfish and Dominofish of varying sizes must be one of the most picturesque sights in the Red Sea. The Anemone will also usually contain its resident beautifully marked cleaner shrimps to add to the scene.

In the aquarium, the Two Bar Anemonefish will feed it's anemone by taking food and ejecting it into the tentacles. I suspect that this activity serves two purposes - firstly to feed the Anemone, but secondly the fish may be using it's host as a personal food store. We have not observed this activity in the wild. The Anemonefish also protects its host from Butterflyfishes which occasionally feed on anemones.

Two Damselfishes appear to be particularly attractive to isopod parasites. The Sulphur, and more frequently the Weber, are often seen hosting one or more parasites. The isopods can be very large in relation to the fish, but do not appear to disadvantage the host to any great extent, except in some very severe cases.

Many Damselfishes adopt camouflage when sleeping at night, or hiding in dark places during the day. The Sergeants are particularly notable, and can become almost totally black, with their normally black bands just showing through. The Black Bordered Dascyllus adopts a very clever disguise, by changing its normally buff coloured body to a dark black/brown, leaving a vertical strip unchanged - this is very effective when hiding in coral branches.

Damselfishes (Pomacentridae)

Amblyglyphidodon	*flavilatus* [1]	*Pomacentrus*	*albicaudatus* [1]
Amblyglyphidodon	*leucogaster*	*Pomacentrus*	*aquilus*
Chrysiptera	*annulata*	*Pomacentrus*	*leptus* [1]
Chrysiptera	*unimaculata*	*Pomacentrus*	*sulfureus*
Neopomacentrus	*cyanomus*	*Pomacentrus*	*trichourus*
Neopomacentrus	*miryae* [1]	*Pomacentrus*	*trilineatus*
Neopomacentrus	*xanthurus* [1]	*Pristotis*	*cyanostigma* [1]
Paraglyphidodon	*melas*	*Stegastes*	*lividus*
Plectroglyphidodon	*lacrymatus*	*Stegastes*	*nigricans*
Plectroglyphidodon	*leucozona cingulum* [1]	*Teixeirichthys*	*jordani*
Chromis	*viridis*	*Dascyllus*	*aruanus*
Chromis	*dimidiata*	*Dascyllus*	*marginatus* [1]
Chromis	*pelloura* [1 2]	*Dascyllus*	*trimaculatus*
Chromis	*pembae*	*Amphiprion*	*bicinctus* [1]
Chromis	*flavaxilla*	*Abudefduf*	*vaigiensis*
Chromis	*trialpha* [1]	*Abudefduf*	*sexfasciatus*
Chromis	*weberi*	*Abudefduf*	*sordidus*

1 Red Sea species

2 *Chromis pelloura* is reported only from the Gulf of Aqaba at depths below 30m.

Twobar Anemonefish *Amphiprion bicinctus*

Size: to 12cm

Red Sea and Gulf of Aden only; hides amongst the tentacles of stoichactid sea anemones.

Rüppell, 1830

Juvenile

Half-and-half Chromis *Chromis dimidiata*

Size: to 9cm

Very common all over coral faces.

Klunzinger, 1871

Arabian Chromis *Chromis flavaxilla*

Size: to 11cm

Common in branching coral on shallow and first shelf reefs. Red Sea and Arabian peninsular form of *C. ternatensis*.

Randall, 1994

Yellow-Edge Chromis *Chromis pembae*

Size: to 13cm

Common at depths of 8m and below.

Smith, 1960

Triplespot Chromis *Chromis trialpha*

Size: to 6cm

Found only in the Red Sea; quite common especially in deeper water along reef faces, and under overhangs.

Allen & Randall, 1981

Bluegreen Chromis *Chromis viridis*

Size: to 9.5cm

Very common on shallow reefs among branching corals. Previously called *C. caerulea*. The breeding male adopts a black dorsal fin and bright yellow soft dorsal and anal rays.

Cuvier, 1830

Weber's Chromis *Chromis weberi*

Size: to 13cm

Common at the 10m level. Frequently hosts isopod parasites, as shown.

Fowler & Bean, 1928

Onespot Damselfish *Chrysiptera unimaculata*

Size: to 8cm

Abundant in shallow areas; juveniles found near coral heads in lagoons.

Cuvier, 1830

Banded Dascyllus *Dascyllus aruanus*

Size: to 7.5cm

Very common; found amongst branching coral in shallow water; sometimes in large groups, although each owning its own territory.

Linnaeus, 1758

Blackbordered Dascyllus *Dascyllus marginatus*

Size: to 6cm

Red Sea to Gulf of Oman; quite common amongst branching corals; in family groups.

Rüppell, 1828

Domino *Dascyllus trimaculatus*

Size: to 14cm

Juveniles often found sharing anemones with the Twobar Anemonefish; adults in loose aggregations at sides of reefs. Adults can be various colours, deep red being one of them.

Rüppell, 1829

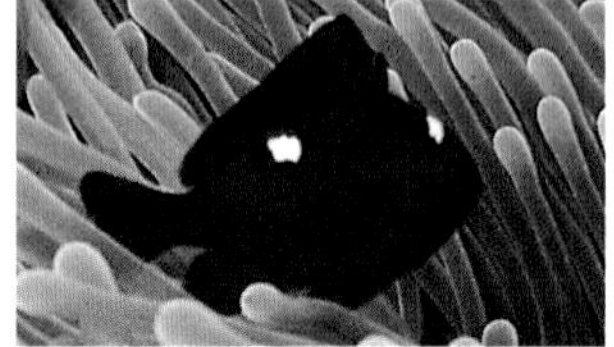

Juvenile

Miry's Damselfish *Neopomacentrus miryae*

Size: to 11cm

Found only in the Red Sea; quite common on top and sides of reefs, sometimes in the company of Anthias.

Dor & Allen, 1977

Red Sea Damselfish *Neopomacentrus xanthurus*

Size: to 8cm

Red Sea to Gulf of Aden.

Allen & Randall, 1981

Royal Damselfish *Paraglyphidodon melas*

Size: to 18cm

Common at sides of reefs and amongst coral heads; juveniles hide in branching coral. Adults can, and will, bite divers.

Cuvier, 1830

Juvenile

Jewel Damselfish *Plectroglyphidodon lacrymatus*

Size: to 11cm

Common, especially in areas of dead coral; strongly territorial.

Quoy & Gaimard, 1825

Whitebar Damselfish *Plectroglyphidodon leucozona cingulum*

Size: to 12cm

The Red Sea form is slightly different from the Indo-Pacific form and is regarded as a separate sub-species.

Klunzinger, 1871

Juvenile

Sombre Damselfish *Pomacentrus aquilus*

Size: to 10cm

Not very common, and difficult to distinguish from other dark coloured damselfishes.

Allen & Randall, 1981

Slender Damselfish *Pomacentrus leptus*

Size: to 6.5cm

Red Sea only; not very common.

Allen & Randall, 1981

Sulphur Damselfish *Pomacentrus sulfureus*

Size: to 10cm

Common, singly along sides of reefs.

Klunzinger, 1871

Reticulated Damselfish *Pomacentrus trichourus*

Size: to 11cm

Common at the 10m level, usually solitary.

Playfair & Gunther, 1866

Juvenile

Threeline Damselfish *Pomacentrus trilineatus*

Size: to 11cm

Common in shallow silty water.

Cuvier, 1830

Juvenile

Dottybacks

Dottybacks are small fish that exhibit the mannerisms and characteristics of their much larger cousins the Groupers. There are 13 species reported in the Red Sea, the most commonly seen by divers being the Orchid Dottyback. Of the 13 species, 7 are endemic to the Red Sea, and surprisingly, were named only recently in the 1960s and 1970s. After the Damselfishes, the Dottyback family (or as they are sometimes known, Basslets) contains the most species that are endemic to the Red Sea.

The beautiful little Orchid Dottyback (usually 5-6cm long) lives on the reef face, invariably below 6m, under overhangs. It is an independently minded fish, but will usually be seen in groups, each individual having its own personal territory. The Orchid Dottyback, since it is seen mostly in deeper water, appears to be all blue, because of the lack of red light at this depth, and shows very prominently against a dark reef face. In fact, its colour is a magnificent rich purple in normal light, much the colour of its floral namesake. Oddly, the top part of its tail fin is very often colourless. It also bears a black stripe through its eyes, and when viewed head-on, it has a very bad-tempered appearance.

Another striking member of the family is the Sunrise Dottyback - light blue with a yellow stripe the length of its body along the dorsal fin. This and other members of the family are more cautious than the Orchid Dottyback, and will only occasionally come out of hiding.

In the shallow areas the Olive Dottyback, light brown tinged with yellow, is the predominant representative of the family. It will be found in small coral formations, and although it is quite numerous, is difficult to see.

Dottybacks survive principally on zooplankton, small worms and crustaceans. Although they tend to agressiveness, their inquisitive nature makes them amusing aquarium fish.

The Dottybacks will often be seen apparently suspended, motionless - they are able to maintain a stationary position with just very delicate fan-like movement of their pectoral and tail fins whatever the current.

Many species of Dottyback exhibit extreme colour forms, which can confuse the amateur identifier. As examples, *P. flavivertex* has an all yellow form and *P. olivaceus* can be a deep brown with red edged fins.

Dottybacks (Pseudochromidae)

Pseudochromis	*dixurus* [1]	*Pseudochromis*	*springeri* [1]
Pseudochromis	*flavivertex* [1]	*Pseudochromis*	*sankeyi* [1]
Pseudochromis	*fridmani* [1]	*Pseudoplesiops*	*lubbocki*
Pseudochromis	*olivaceus* [1]	*Chlidichthys*	*rubiceps*
Pseudochromis	*pesi* [1]	*Chlidichthys*	*auratus* [1]
		Haliophis	*guttatus*

1 Red Sea species

Black Damselfish *Stegastes nigricans*

Size: to 13cm

Very common in shallow water and areas of dead reef and rubble; very aggressive and will bite; *S. lividus* is similar in appearance but is very rare.

Lacepède, 1802

Forktail Dottyback *Pseudochromis dixurus*

Size: to 9cm

Endemic to the Red Sea. Found in dark reef face crevices or under overhangs, usually below 20m. Not common. The lateral stripe is often very dark, giving this fish an overall brown colour.

Lubbock, 1975

Sunrise Dottyback *Pseudochromis flavivertex*

Size: 35cm

Red Sea and Gulf of Aden. Seen in sheltered, often sandy areas amongst coral.

Rüppell, 1835

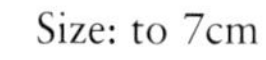

Orchid Dottyback *Pseudochromis fridmani*

Size: to 7cm

Seen in groups, each with its own territory, usually below 10m. Red Sea species.

Klausewitz, 1968

Olive Dottyback *Pseudochromis olivaceus*

Size: to 9cm

Red Sea to Arabian Gulf. Commonly found in coral heads, usually in shallow water. Additional photo shows different colour form - dark brown with red edged fins. Rarely observed below 10m.

Rüppell, 1835

Pale Dottyback *Pseudochromis pesi*

Size: to 10cm

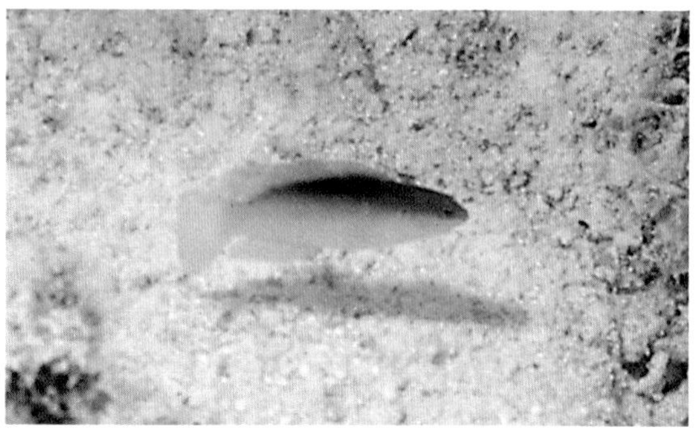

Reported in Gulf of Aqaba only, but this photograph was taken off Hurgada, north east Egypt.

Lubbock, 1975

Emperors & Sea Bream

Emperors are well represented in the Red Sea, with 16 of the 20 Indo Pacific region species being present. They have some similar physical characteristics to their relatives the Snappers, Grunts and Sea Breams, but can generally be identified by their more pointed snouts. Specific identification of Emperors can be difficult, which perhaps accounts for the frequent renaming of species. Their colours are usually inconspicuous, but when alarmed they may show yellow, blue or green coloured areas, and broad vertical bands; this characteristic is most noticeable in the Mahsena Emperor.

Generally their colouration as juveniles is uninteresting; an exception is the Bigeye Emperor juvenile which bears four wide black vertical bands on a silver white background on the top half of its body and bright yellow edging to its tail fin.

Emperors are nocturnal by nature, but do not appear to make an effort to hide during the day - often they will be seen apparently aimlessly wandering in the open water off the reef - it is likely, however, that they are watching the sand below for movement, in anticipation of a meal of mollusc.

Although we do not believe that they are territorial, we have noticed that young Emperors will often be seen in a particular favourite location, week after week.

Their diet is composed chiefly of molluscs, which they obtain by crushing shells with their strong stubby teeth. Some species particularly enjoy sea urchins, and may sometimes bear the pinprick evidence of attacks on these creatures around their snouts.

Emperors are large fish, some species attaining 100cm in length. They are excellent to eat, and will always be seen in the local markets.

Sea Breams, much like the Emperors, are slow moving, aimlessly wandering fish, often seen in small schools. Also like the Emperors they have low mouths and feed on molluscs and crustaceans. A recreational diver is only likely to see 3 of the 14 species reported in the Red Sea. Sea Bream are very shiny fish when seen in clear water - their preferred habitat, however, appears to be murky areas with sandy bottoms - this must follow from their liking for molluscs.

Emperors (Lethrinidae)	
Gymnocranius	*grandoculis*[2]
Lethrinus	*borbonicus*
Lethrinus	*microdon*
Lethrinus	*harak*
Lethrinus	*lentjan*
Lethrinus	*mahsena*
Lethrinus	*nebulosus*
Lethrinus	*obsoletus*
Lethrinus	*olivaceus*
Lethrinus	*variegatus*
Lethrinus	*xanthochilus*
Monotaxis	*grandoculis*

Sea Bream (Porgies)	(Sparidae)
Acanthopagrus	*bifasciatus*
Crenidens	*crenidens*
Rhabdosargus	*sarba*
Argyrops	*spinifer*
Diplodus	*noct*[1]
Acanthopagrus	*berda*

1 Red Sea species
2 Deep water species

Bluestriped Dottyback *Pseudochromis springeri*

Size: to 6cm

Red Sea only. Seen singly always in coral. A small species, not common in the Jeddah area.

Lubbock, 1975

Blackspot Emperor *Lethrinus harak*

Size: to 50cm

Common near inner reefs and in sandy lagoons.

Forsskål, 1775

Redspot Emperor *Lethrinus lentjan*

Size: to 40cm

Seen over sandy bottoms near reefs down to 50m.

Lacepède, 1802

Mahsena Emperor *Lethrinus mahsena*

Size: to 50cm

Very common in inshore waters. It can change rapidly from plain silver to a barred pattern. Sometimes sports a yellow patch on caudal peduncle.

Forsskål, 1775

Redfin Emperor *Lethrinus borbonicus*

Size: to 30cm

Fairly common. It can adopt yellow stripes at will.

Valenciennes, 1830

Spangled Emperor *Lethrinus nebulosus*

Size: to 80cm

Common at dive sites on the north west coast, rarely seen along Jeddah coast. The blue markings are not so clear on younger individuals.

Forsskål, 1775

Sub-adult

Yellowstripe Emperor *Lethrinus obsoletus*

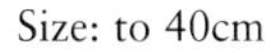

Size: to 40cm

In older individuals a yellow stripe can be seen at the level of the pectoral fin. This stripe can be displayed at will. Previously known as *L. ramak*.

Forsskål, 1775

Variegated Emperor *Lethrinus variegatus*

Size: to 20cm

Not common.

Valenciennes, 1830

Yellowlip Emperor *Lethrinus xanthochilus*

Size: to 60cm

Solitary, not common, difficult to approach. Near seaward reefs, and in lagoons. Very prominent yellow lower lip in mature individuals.

Klunzinger, 1870

Bigeye Emperor *Monotaxis grandoculis*

Size: to 60cm

Very common in small groups hovering at side of reef; broad band of juvenile stage persists to 20-25cm size.

Forsskål, 1775

Doublebar Bream *Acanthopagrus bifasciatus*

Size: to 50cm

Hovers at the side of reefs in small groups; more common on the west side of the Red Sea.

Forsskål, 1775

Lunar Fusilier *Caesio lunaris*

Size: to 30cm

Seen in large schools near edge of reef, over deep water.

Ehrenberg, 1830

Fusiliers

The Fusiliers are the elegant, active, fishes that are frequently seen in the open water just off the fringing reef. They are sleek and silvery, have forked tails, and usually form large schools as they feed on planktonic material. They are closely allied to the Snappers, and are sometimes classified in the same family. They are diurnal, and at night they will be found along the reef edge suspended in sleep.

There are 4 species commonly seen in the Red Sea (11 reported), none of which grows larger than about 30cm. The smallest species is the Goldband Fusilier, which can form huge schools and can often be mistaken for Sardine.

Very often when a large school of these fish is seen they will contain a mix of species - we have observed a particular school containing 3 species of Fusiliers.

Juvenile Fusiliers will often be seen shoaling with Anthias on coral pinnacles - they are often the prey of passing Jacks.

Fusiliers (Caesionidae)

Caesio	*lunaris*	*Caesio*	*suevicus*[1]
Caesio	*striatus*	*Caesio*	*xanthonota*
Caesio	*caerulaurea*	*Pterocaesio*	*chrysozona*

1 Red Sea Species

Goatfishes

The Goatfishes' claim to fame is that it is one of the few species of Indo Pacific region fishes that has migrated through the Suez Canal to the Mediterranean Sea.

There are approximately 60 species worldwide and 14 are known in the Red Sea.

It may appear to divers that 14 is an underestimate, since some species can alter their colours and markings quite substantially; the Yellowsaddle Goatfish is a typical example. This fish can at one time be entirely dark blue or bright yellow, at another the more familiar yellow/silver colour.

The main characteristic of Goatfishes is their ability to sift through the sandy sea bed using two long barbels to find food. The barbels perform two functions - primarily as sensors they 'taste' potential food, and whilst doing so they disturb the sand thereby revealing more potential food. They are so successful that, as soon as they agitate the sand and a sand cloud forms, other fish, typically Wrasses, crowd around for a free meal. Goatfish are unaggressive, and will allow any number of scroungers to join in. Sometimes roles are reversed - Goatfish will be seen scavenging after larger Wrasses, such as the Rockmover, which can cause considerable disturbance to the sea floor.

Striated Fusilier *Caesio striatus*

Size: to 18cm

Form large schools off reef sides.

Rüppell, 1830

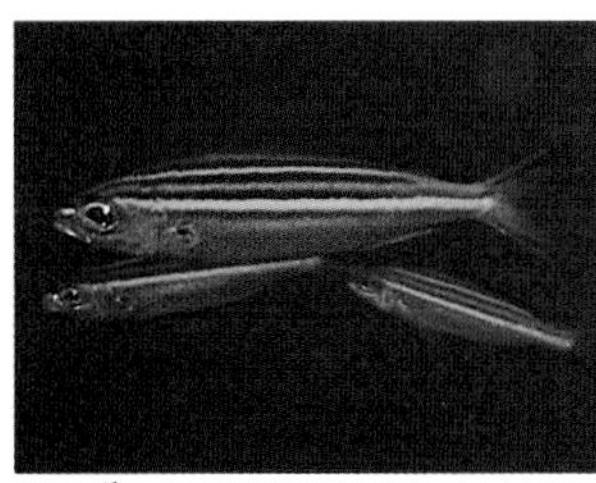

Juvenile

Suez Fusilier *Caesio suevicus*

Size: to 25cm

Endemic to the Red Sea, found in large schools often mixed with *C. lunaris*.

Klunzinger, 1884

Yellowstripe Goatfish *Mulloidichthys flavolineatus*

Size: to 40cm

Often in large schools by day. Prefers sandy areas.

Lacepède, 1802

Yellowfin Goatfish *Mulloidichthys vanicolensis*

Size: to 38cm

Quite common. Often seen in large groups along the side of a reef.

Valenciennes, 1831

Yellowsaddle Goatfish *Parupeneus cyclostomus*

Size: to 50cm

The largest Goatfish in the Red Sea. Only smaller individuals show the bright yellow phase. Pinkish colour believed to be common in deep water individuals.

Lacepède, 1801

Forsskål's Goatfish *Parupeneus forsskåli*

Size: to 28cm

Red Sea and Gulf of Aden - common over sandy areas.

Fourmanoir & Gueze, 1976

Long-barbel Goatfish *Parupeneus macronema*

Size: to 30cm

Very common, singly or in groups.

Lacepède, 1801

Juvenile

Rosy Goatfish *Parupeneus rubescens*

Size: to 30cm

Sometimes exhibits a rosy hue on the bottom part of body.

Lacepède, 1801

Steinitz's Goby *Amblyeleotris steinitzi*

Size: to 10cm

Quite common in burrows (sometimes sharing) in sandy bottom associated with an Alpheid shrimp.
Easily confused with *A. sungami*

Klausewitz, 1974

Some species form large schools, most notably the Yellowfin Goatfish, but usually they are seen singularly or in small groups.

At night, their energy spent, they will 'collapse' on the bottom sand without burying themselves or making any attempt to hide.

Goatfishes have two entirely separate dorsal fins; this characteristic, combined with the presence of the barbels make them easily identifiable.

Goatfish (Mullidae)

Mulloidichthys	*flavolineatus*	*Parupeneus*	*cyclostomus*
Mulloidichthys	*vanicolensis*	*Parupeneus*	*forsskali*[1]
Parupeneus	*macronema*	*Parupeneus*	*heptacanthus*
Parupeneus	*rubescens*	*Upeneus*	*tragula*
		Upeneus	*pori*

1 Red Sea species

Gobies & Dartfishes

The family Gobiidae forms the largest group of marine fishes, composed of what may be 1,000 different species worldwide. Gobies constitute a successful family that includes some of the smallest and most versatile creatures in the marine and estuarine environment. The well-known Mudskipper, which survives out of the water for short periods is one of the best examples of versatility. There are in the Red Sea some very small species, typically the Whip Gobies, and species in the Genera *Trimma* and *Eviota*, which are not much more than two centimetres in length, and to make matters worse for the amateur identifier, some are almost transparent. There must be many opportunities to discover new species in the Red Sea - the prime requisite for the aspiring discoverer is good eyesight! Currently there are about 96 recognised species of Goby in the Red Sea.

All Gobies have two separate dorsal fins, and most have fused pelvic fins which help them to perch on sand or coral with their heads held high.

Generally the marine Gobies are solitary (they will sometimes be seen in pairs), bottom dwelling and prefer sandy or silty areas. Certain individual species prefer the protection of coral, and some of these species do not conform to the usually dull coloured Goby stereotype seen on the bottom. Amongst these are the Citron Gobies - the most commonly seen in the Red Sea is bright yellow with blue markings and is easy to spot in branches of Acropoca coral, its preferred habitat. Usually they inhabit a coral head as a family. Another (less likely to be seen, although probably more common) is green with red markings (*Gobiodon rivulatus*). This little Goby may be found by diligently searching isolated shallow area coral heads which it often shares with Banded Dascyllus. The authors have also observed *Gobiodon reticulatus* sharing a coral head with the *G. rivulatus* - this

Tailspot Goby *Amblygobius albimaculatus*

Size: to 17cm

Very common and conspicuous over sandy bottoms. Exhibits a pale colour phase and a dark colour phase. Feeds by sifting sand for invertebrates and algae. Closely related to *A. phalaena* of the Pacific.

Rüppell, 1830

Hector's Goby *Amblygobius hectori*

Size: to 6cm

Common over sand patches amongst coral. Hovers with a characteristic jerky forward and backward movement.

Smith, 1956

Novice Goby *Coryphopterus neophytus*

Size: to 7cm

Found over sandy bottom, near reefs. Previously classed in genus *Fusigobius*.

Günther, 1877

particular Goby is very difficult to see, being dark brown with reddish coloured head. It hides under the coral head, so is seldom noticed.

Hector's Goby (*Amblygobius hectori*) is also a colourful Goby which bears bright yellow lateral stripes on a black body and an eyespot rear dorsally. It will usually be found hovering a few inches above a sandy area within the reef, and is quite common.

The great majority of Gobies live on the bottom, and will invariably be found in sand or the less attractive areas of rubble and silt. They construct burrows for protection and breeding, outside which they will perch, keeping a sharp lookout for a potential meal which could take the form of a small crustacean or simply vegetable matter. They will not stray far from home, and rely on their excellent camouflage for protection. Some of these Gobies (which are often called 'Partner Gobies'), such as the Whitecap, share their burrows with an Alpheid Shrimp, which performs a housecleaning function in return for protection. The shrimp, which is almost blind, uses its antennae to maintain contact with the Goby, and reacts to danger as the Goby reacts. Gobies appear to be very tolerant of other species, and will often be seen sharing a burrow with another type of Goby. We once observed a Whitecap Goby (*Lotilia gracilosa*) sharing its burrow with another unidentified Goby, a Blue Striped Pipefish and of course its usual Alpheid Shrimp companion.

A closely related family is the Microdesmidae, the Dartfishes (or Dartgobies). A number of species in this small family have only very recently been recorded as present in the Red Sea - the most often seen is *Ptereleotris evides*. It will be observed, usually in pairs but sometimes in small groups, 'hovering' at about one metre above the bottom on the first shelf. We have observed a large group of young Dartfish in silty, shallow water.

The Red Sea contains a number of small Gobies, which are numerous but not often noticed. They are often brightly coloured and elaborately patterned. Amongst these are the Whip Gobies, which live on Whip coral and those in the *Eviota* and *Trimma* genera. There is very little available information on these tiny creatures - the identifications used in this book may be inaccurate, since much research needs to be done to classify these fishes.

Gobies (Gobiidae)

Amblyeleotris steinitzi
Amblyeleotris sungami
Amblygobius albimaculatus
Amblygobius hectori
Asterropteryx semipunctatus
Bathygobius cyclopterus
Bathygobius fuscus
Bryaninops natans
Bryaninops yongei
Fusigobius longispinus
Gnatholepis anjerensis
Gobiodon citrinus
Gobiodon rivulatus
Gobiodon reticulatus
Istigobius decoratus
Istigobius ornatus
Lotilia gracilosa
Luposicya lupus

Blue & red-spotted Goby *Cryptocentrus caeruleopunctatus*

Size: 13cm

A Red Sea species living with Alpheid shrimp: not very common.

Rüppell, 1830

Luther's Goby *Cryptocentrus lutheri*

Size: to 11cm

Red Sea to Arabian Gulf, associated with Alpheid shrimp; not common.

Klausewitz, 1960

Halfspotted Goby *Asterropteryx semipunctatus*

Size: to 5cm

Lives in areas of dead reef, in shallow water. Photographed in the authors' aquarium.

Rüppell, 1830

Purpleeye Goby *Bryaninops natans*

Size: to 2.5cm

Hover in groups over coral. This small species can easily be mistaken for fry of other fishes.

Larson, 1985

Whip Goby *Bryaninops yongei*

Size: to 3cm

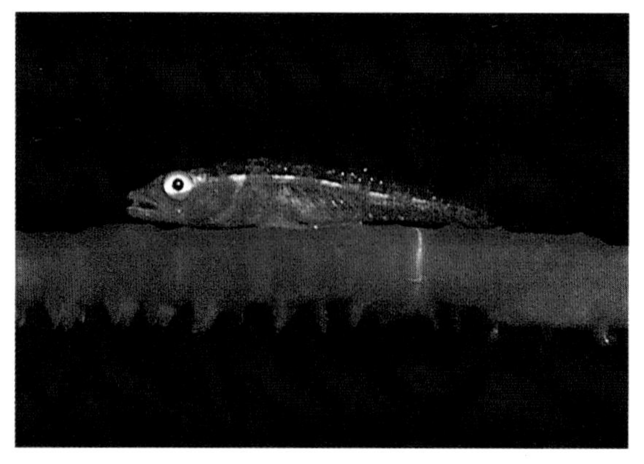

Found on Whip coral. When approached hides on the opposite side of the coral.

Davis & Cohen, 1968

Goby *Cryptocentrus sp.*

The blue spots on body and the shape of the dorsal fin suggest *Cryptocentrus* genus.

Orange-lined Prawn Goby *Ctenogobiops crocineus*

Size:to 7cm

Associated with Alpheid shrimp; not common.

Smith, 1959

Sandy Prawn Goby *Ctenogobiops feroculus*

Size: to 6cm

More likely found at second shelf level, in sandy areas.

Lubbock & Polunin, 1977

Prawn Goby *Ctenogobiops maculosus*

Size: to 7cm

Red Sea only, associated with Alpheid shrimp; common.

Fourmanoir, 1955

Spotted Dwarf Goby *Eviota guttata*

Size: to 2.5cm

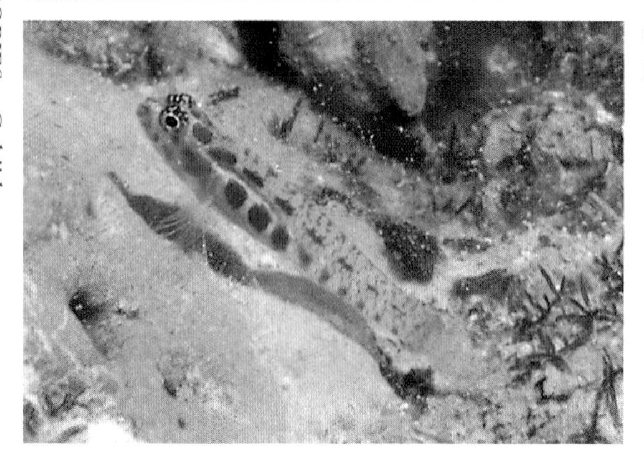

Common, but difficult to find.

Lachner & Karnella, 1978

Redstripe Dwarf Goby *Eviota sebreei*

Size: to 3cm

A common species most often seen below the first shelf at below 15m.

Jordan & Seale, 1906

Dwarf Goby *Eviota sp.*

Similar to *E. sebreei*, but with different markings.

Eye-bar Goby *Gnatholepis anjerensis*

Size: to 8cm

Prefers sandy areas at base of coral. Often in groups.

Bleeker, 1851

Citron Goby *Gobiodon citrinus*

Size: to 6cm

Lives in branches of live coral (especially Acropora), in family groups. Fairly common and easily seen.

Rüppell, 1828

Redhead Goby *Paragobiodon echinocephalus*

Size: to 3.5cm

A fairly common Goby found on the underside of Stylophora coral heads in shallow water. Its head bears short bristles. It is extremely difficult to find. Photographed in authors' aquarium.

Rüppell, 1830

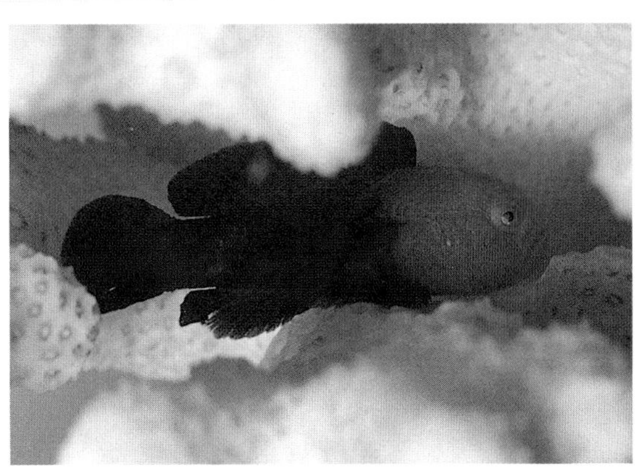

Rivulate Goby *Gobiodon rivulatus*

Size: to 6cm

Found in isolated coral heads, fairly common but not often seen.

Rüppell, 1828

Decorated Goby *Istigobius decoratus*

Size: to 12cm

Common in sandy lagoons.

Herre, 1927

Ornate Goby Istigobius ornatus

Size: to 10cm

Seen in sandy lagoons, usually at the base of coral heads.

Rüppell, 1830

Whitecap Goby *Lotilia graciliosa*

Size: to 5cm

Associated with Alpheid shrimp. Prefers sandy holes at the base of reefs.

Klausewitz, 1960

Michel's Goby *Pleurosicya micheli*

Size: to 2.5cm

Common on live coral, or sponge.

Fourmanoir, 1971

Dwarf Goby *Trimma avidori*

Size: about 3cm

A common small Goby seen usually below 15m. Stations itself on coral, darting up to take passing zooplankton.

Goren, 1978

Dwarf Goby *Trimma flavicaudatus*

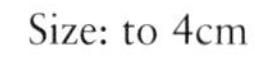
Size: to 4cm

Invariably stationed vertically on a reef face, waiting for passing zooplankton.

Goren, 1982

Dwarf Goby *Trimma sp.*

The author is unable to identify this species, although it is not uncommon. Size shown is approximately 3.5cm.

Maiden Goby *Valenciennea puellaris*

Size: to 14cm

Lives in burrows in sandy areas, usually in pairs.

Tomiyama, 1956

Sixspot Goby *Valenciennea sexguttata*

Size: to 14cm

Lives in sand burrows. Usually seen in pairs, sometimes in small groups.

Valenciennes, 1837

Twotone Dartfish *Ptereleotris evides*

Size: to 15cm

Often seen over sandy areas, large adults in pairs, juveniles often in groups.

Jordan & Hubbs, 1925

Spot tail Dartfish *Ptereleotris heteroptera*

Size: to 12cm

Hovers, usually in pairs, over sandy areas.

Bleeker, 1855

Coryphopterus neophytus
Cryptocentrus caeruleopunctatus[1]
Cryptocentrus lutheri
Ctenogobiops feroculus
Ctenogobiops maculosus[1]
Cryptocentrus cryptocentrus
Discordipinna griessingeri
Eviota guttata
Eviota prasina
Eviota sebreei
Oplopomus oplopomus
Paragobiodon echinocephalus
Pleurosicya micheli
Trimma avidori
Trimma flavicaudatus
Valenciennea puellaris
Valenciennea sexguttata
Valenciennea wardii
Vanderhorstia mertensi

Dartfishes (Microdesmidae)
Ptereleotris microlepis
Ptereleotris evides
Ptereleotris heteroptera
Ptereleotris arabica[1]
Ptereleotris zebra[2]

1 Red Sea species 2 Southern Red Sea only

Groupers, Anthias & Soapfishes

The Groupers form one of the largest groups of reef fishes present in the Red Sea. One of its members, Anthias, has some claim to giving the Sea its name.

Although Anthias are part of the Grouper family and Soapfishes are close relatives, the general conception of Groupers is of the fine eating fish of the *Epinephelus* genus. Groupers of this genus are characterised by huge mouths contributing to a rather fearsome appearance and are voracious predators of other fish. Some species can grow to enormous size, up to 2m long and 200kg in weight. Unfortunately they are easy targets for spearfishermen, since they are not usually nervous of divers - the larger specimens have little to fear from other predators. It is indeed an awesome experience to come face to face with a 100kg fish in a cave or wreck, but it is not dangerous and will not threaten man. Groupers actually have very small teeth, with which they grind their catch.

Groupers are territorial, and some species spend most of their time idly resting on their pelvic fins outside their lair, waiting for dinner to come to them.

The sex life of the Groupers is complex - some species can be male and female simultaneously, and can perform as either, but self fertilisation does not occur - spawning pairs fertilise each others eggs. Although generally starting life as female, they can adopt either sex - a sure way to perpetuate the species.

The most often seen in the Red Sea are the Coral, Peacock and Half spotted Groupers.

A remarkable characteristic of Groupers is their ability to change their colour and body patterns - in some cases even reverse their colours. The variety of

Pale Dartfish *Ptereleotris microlepis*

Size: to 12cm

Hovers over sandy areas near reefs, often in groups.

Bleeker, 1856

Redmouth Grouper *Aethaloperca rogaa*

Size: to 60cm

Quite common; easily recognised by its deep body shape.

Forsskål, 1775

Adult

Subadult

Slender Grouper *Anyperodon leucogrammicus*

Size: to 50cm

Very elusive; not very common; often in pairs. Juveniles with orangeish stripes and blue edged black spot at back of dorsal fin and base of tail - believed to mimic a species of Wrasse.

Valenciennes, 1838

disguises adopted by the Blacktip Grouper is particularly notable - at one time it can be an overall drab buff colour, at the next it will be silvery with blood red tears under its eyes.

The identification of the mature Groupers is sometimes quite difficult - particularly of those in the *Epinephelus* genus. They all tend to become an overall dark colour, with darker spots.

The scenic underwater photographs that one sees in travel brochures advertising the Red Sea invariably contain a multitude of little red fishes usually shown over magnificent coral formations. These are the Scalefin Anthias that are so well associated with the Sea's coral reefs.

When studied, these photographs will show a smaller number of pinkish coloured Anthias amongst a much greater number of bright red individuals. The pinkish males preside over a harem of females, and usually maintain a position slightly above the females. The harem will contain a pecking order, and should the male be lost, the dominant female will change sex and assume the male role.

The two species of Anthias most often seen in the Red Sea are commonly called the Scalefin and the Striped - the Scalefin is by far the more numerous. We have not observed the Striped Anthias in the central east coast area, but they are fairly numerous in the northern area, very often seen amongst aggregations of its Scalefin cousins.

Three other species of *Pseudanthias* have been reported to be in the Red Sea - the Redstripe (*P. fasciatus*) and Heemstra's (*P. heemstrai*), and only recently *P. lunulatus* has been reported - but none of these three have been observed by the authors.

Soapfishes, which are represented by 3 species in the Red Sea, are so called for the toxic mucus which covers them. The two representatives, the Goldstripe and the Yellowface, do not grow to any great size. The Goldstripe is common, and will be found in dense coral formations, and very often in silty colourless areas of reef. This particular species develops its stripes as it grows older, a juvenile having only four white stripes on its black body background.

The Yellowface Soapfish is also fairly common, more so at depths below 20m, and will be found hiding in the dark recesses of the reef face.

Soapfishes are sometimes classified as a sub-family of the Serranidae or put into a separate family Grammistidae.

Groupers (Serranidae)

Aethaloperca	*rogaa*
Anyperodon	*leucogrammicus*
Cephalopholis	*argus*
Cephalopholis	*hemistiktos*
Cephalopholis	*miniata*
Cephalopholis	*oligosticta*[1]

Soapfish (Sub-family, Grammistinae)

Aulacocephalus	*temmincki*[3]
Diploprion	*drachi*[1]
Grammistes	*sexlineatus*

1 Red Sea species 2 Southern Red Sea 3 Deep water species

Peacock Grouper *Cephalopholis argus*

Size: to 50cm

Mostly solitary or in pairs; seldom leaves the protection of coral. The second photograph shows the strongly coloured sub-adult.

Bloch & Schneider, 1801

Halfspotted Grouper *Cephalopholis hemistiktos*

Size: to 35cm

Red Sea to Arabian Gulf only; most common species in the Red Sea; all colour forms exhibit iridescent blue tail edging.

Rüppell, 1830

Coral Grouper *Cephalopholis miniata*

Size: to 40cm

Common, peeking out from amongst the coral. Juveniles yellow with scattered spots. Bands can be turned on and off at will.

Forsskål, 1775

Vermillion Grouper *Cephalopholis oligosticta*

Size: to 30cm

Similar to C. *miniata*, but much deeper body. A Red Sea species that is very shy and not often observed. It will be found in dark caves and crevices at 20-30m.

Randall & Ben Tuvia, 1982

Sixspot Grouper *Cephalopholis sexmaculata*

Size: to 50cm

Found in dark caves, usually paired.

Rüppell, 1830

Brownspotted Grouper *Epinephelus chlorostigma*

Size: to 75cm

Not very common.

Valenciennes, 1828

Blacktip Grouper *Epinephelus fasciatus*

Size: to 35cm

Quite common; black tips of dorsal spines persist in all colour forms.

Forsskål, 1775

Brownmarbled Grouper *Epinephelus fuscoguttatus*

Size: to 90cm

Not very common.

Forsskål, 1775

Summana Grouper *Epinephelus summana*

Size: to 50cm

Red Sea to Gulf of Aden only; near shallow reefs and lagoons.

Forsskål, 1775

Greasy Grouper *Epinephelus tauvina*

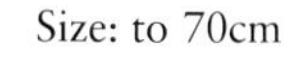

Size: to 70cm

Perhaps the most commonly seen of the large groupers. Often, 5 faint bars may be seen on the body.

Forsskål, 1775

Potato Grouper *Epinephelus tukula*

Size: to 140cm

Clear water species. (*E. fuscoguttatus* in background). Photo Hurghada.

Morgans, 1959

Squaretail Grouper *Plectropomus areolatus*

Size: to 100cm

Active during the day, found at about 20m. Reported to aggregate when spawning.

Rüppell, 1828

Red Sea Coral Cod *Plectropomus pessuliferus marisrubri*

Size: to 110cm

Red Sea and Gulf of Aden only; more common in the northern Red Sea.

Fowler, 1904

Lunartail Grouper *Variola louti*

Size: to 80cm

Quite common near all reefs but usually of moderate size only. Larger individuals do not exhibit bands.

Forsskål, 1775

Juvenile

Scalefin Anthias *Pseudanthias squamipinnis*

Size: to 12cm

Female

Male

Common on all reefs, always in groups. Males maintain harems, but often males and females will be seen in separate groups.

Peters, 1855

Cephalopholis	*sexmaculata*
Dermatolepsis	*striolatus*[2]
Epinephelus	*areolatus*
Epinephelus	*chlorostigma*
Epinephelus	*fasciatus*
Epinephelus	*fuscoguttatus*
Epinephelus	*latifasciatus*
Epinephelus	*malabaricus*
Epinephelus	*lanceolatus*
Epinephelus	*polyphekadion*
Epinephelus	*morrhua*
Epinephelus	*episticus*
Epinephelus	*stoliczkae*
Epinephelus	*summana*[1]
Epinephelus	*tauvina*
Epinephelus	*radiatus*
Epinephelus	*tukula*
Plectropomus	*pessuliferus marisrubri*[1]
Plectropomus	*areolatus*
Variola	*louti*

Anthias

Pseudanthias	*squamipinnis*
Pseudanthias	*taeniatus*[1]
Pseudanthias	*fasciatus*
Pseudanthias	*heemstrai*[1]
Pseudanthias	*lunulatus*

1 Red Sea species 2 Southern Red Sea 3 Deep water species

Hawkfishes

The most commonly seen of the Hawkfishes is the Blackside Hawkfish. They are the ever present, motionless predators that perch on a coral ledge waiting for the opportunity to seize a small passing fish. They appear to alter their colour and colour pattern to suit their surroundings - despite their name they can appear yellow with reddish markings.

Of the 35 species known to exist in the Indo Pacific region, only 4 are seen in the Red Sea.

The Blackside will usually be observed on the top, along the face and at the base of the fringing reef, whilst the largest of the Hawkfishes, the Stocky Hawkfish will only be seen on top of the reef. This latter fish blends so well into its surroundings, that despite its size, it is often difficult to see in the changing light conditions of the turbulent water on the reef.

Often when photographing fish we have unintentionally included a small Pixy Hawkfish in the frame. These are the pretty red blotched little predators that are very common, but frequently overlooked as they remain motionless in their vantage points below coral heads or on dark ledges. Once when diving on a mature wreck, we were surprised to find a Pixie Hawkfish in every nook and

Striped Anthias *Pseudanthias taeniatus*

Size: to 13cm

Male

Female

Seen in groups, sometimes mixed with Scalefin Anthias. More common in northern areas.

Klunzinger, 1884

Yellowface Soapfish *Diploprion drachi*

Size: to 14cm

Red Sea to Gulf of Aden only. Not very common - usually seen at about 10m and below.

Estève, 1955

Goldstriped Soapfish *Grammistes sexlineatus*

Size: to 25cm

Common in crevices and under ledges often in shallow silty water. Juveniles have fewer lateral stripes; a juvenile is shown devouring a Chromis.

Thunberg, 1792

cranny, repeatedly defending its territory against intrusion by its neighbours. On the hull of the wreck, the Pixie Hawkfish population must have been at least six per square metre!

Finally, the Longnose Hawkfish, a favourite of photographers and aquarists, is unfortunately found usually at depths greater than 30m; it will often position itself on a gorgonian or branch of black coral. It has been reported at 20m.

Hawkfishes (Cirrhitidae)	
Cirrhitichthys	*oxycephalus*
Cirrhitus	*pinnulatus*
Oxycirrhites	*typus*
Paracirrhites	*forsteri*

Longfins

Longfins, as their name suggests, have unusually large fins - both the dorsal and anal fins meet the tail fin to give the fish the appearance of being much larger than it actually is. The pelvic fins also are disproportionate, being almost half the length of the body.

Of the three species of Longfin known in the Red Sea, only one is likely to be seen, and that rarely. Known as the Comet (*Calloplesiops altivelis*), it is most often observed at dusk cautiously leaving its hiding place in the reef face. It is unmistakable in appearance with a blue/black body and longitudinal white spots. It has wide flowing fins and an oval-shaped tail, also covered in white spots.

The Comet is a very shy fish, and if subjected to the glare of a torch at night, will retreat into the reef face, head first and rather slowly. This manner of retreat has been described as an imitation of the way that a particular Moray Eel (*Gymnothorax meleagris*) retreats into its lair. The Comet will leave its tail slightly protruding from the reef, and at first glance, could be mistaken for the head of a Moray. The white spotted tail mimics the appearance of the Moray's head. The illusion is enhanced by the presence of a blue-edged eye spot at the rear base of the Comet's dorsal fin.

The Whitespotted Longfin (*Plesiops nigricans*) has only been observed by the authors in very shallow water, and it was well hidden in a bed of seagrass.

Plesiops caeruleolineatus is, like the Comet, nocturnal. Being also a small fish (up to 8cm) it is unlikely to be often seen.

Longfins (Plesiopidae)	
Plesiops	*caeruleolineatus*
Calloplesiops	*altivelis*
Plesiops	*nigricans*[1]

1 Red Sea species

Pixy Hawkfish *Cirrhitichthys oxycephalus*

Size: to 8.5cm

Common; found amongst coral branches and reef crevices.

Bleeker, 1855

Stocky Hawkfish *Cirrhitus pinnulatus*

Size: to 28cm

Common on reef tops. The largest of the Hawkfishes.

Bloch & Schneider, 1801

Longnose Hawkfish *Oxycirrhites typus*

Size: to 13cm

Not common above 20m. This individual (6cm) was, however, photographed at 15m.

Bleeker, 1857

Blackside Hawkfish *Paracirrhites forsteri*

Size: to 22cm

Very common, often seen fully exposed on coral outcrops. Two colour variants shown.

Bloch & Schneider, 1801

Comet *Calloplesiops altivelis*

Size: to 16cm

Not common; appears from its hide at dusk.

Steindachner, 1903

Whitespotted Longfin *Plesiops nigricans*

Size: to 12cm

A shallow-water species preferring a seagrass environment.
Photo - authors' aquarium

Rüppell, 1828

Parrotfishes

The Parrotfishes are very deserving of their name - like their namesakes in the avarian world they are gaudy and gregarious creatures and sport a parrotlike beak (formed by fused teeth) designed to break hard material. These multicoloured, active, fishes are present on all the reefs busily feeding during the daylight hours. Akin to the Wrasses, they show many similar characteristics in the way they swim (using their pectoral fins) and their early to bed and late to rise behaviour.

Parrotfishes are a challenge to the amateur identifier. Snorkellers and divers swimming along a fringing reef will be aware of many of these fish busily going about their business, no two looking the same. Their colours and colour patterns change remarkedly according to age, circumstances and sex (all Parrotfishes change sex, except the shallow-water species *L. vaigiensis*). Juveniles are often colourful with lateral stripes or spots - there is usually no suggestion of the adult colours. The authors have been unable to find authoritative descriptions of all the juvenile parrotfishes.

The post-juvenile stage of development (called the initial phase) produces usually drab brownish colour overall and indeterminate sex (usually female), and when they become sexually active they adopt the familiar blue/green colouration (some, however, may contain orange or red). Old terminal males are often brightly coloured, blue and green being predominant.

Parrotfish are characterised by their fused teeth, which enable them to scrape off algae and the soft parts of coral formations. They will often break the hard coral to get at the polyps and algae inside. The process of breaking off and grinding hard coral is a major contributor to the accumulation of fine sand and sediment found around coral reefs.

The colour of the teeth of Parrotfish can help identification of species - some species will have red, and others blue teeth, whilst others will have shades of these colours.

Daytime in the Red Sea is a noisy place, and it is the Parrotfishes who contribute much to the mysterious clicks and clacks one hears. The authors were fortunate to witness a school of some 20 Bumphead Parrotfishes grazing the fringing reef off Port Sudan. These huge fish created a fearful din, suggesting gunfire and an imminent marine revolution!

Bumpheads are not often seen along the Saudi Arabian coastline; they are rather shy fish and we have only seen them in small numbers or solitary - we have observed a single Bumphead keeping company with a family of at least 8 small Humphead (or Napolean) Wrasses; by weight, I estimated that the Bumphead was four times the weight of the largest Napolean!

An unusual night-time characteristic of some Parrotfish is their ability to surround themselves with a mucus lining, giving the appearance of a translucent balloon, when sleeping in a coral crevice. It is assumed that this lining is an advance warning device to warn of approaching predators, which may include a Moray eel or a cone shell mollusc.

Bumphead Parrotfish *Bolbometopon muricatum*

Size: to 120cm

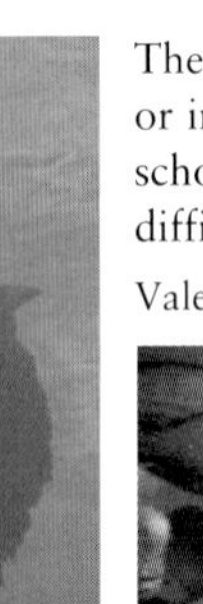

The largest species, seen singly or in pairs. Sometimes in large schools. They are very difficult to approach.

Valenciennes, 1840

Dotted Parrotfish *Calotomus viridescens*

Size: to 27cm

Terminal male

One of the smaller species, found only in the Red Sea. Mostly solitary, prefers sandy areas.

Rüppell, 1835

Initial phase

Bicolour Parrotfish *Cetoscarus bicolor*

Size: to 80cm

Terminal male

Large species. Initial phase easy to identify, with thick yellow lateral stripe.

Rüppell, 1829

Initial phase

Purplestreak Parrotfish *Chlorurus genazonatus*

Size: to 30cm

Red Sea and Gulf of Aden only. Common around fringing reef. Initial phase brown with orangeish bars on scales. Previously placed in Genus *Scarus*.

Randall & Bruce, 1983

Steepheaded Parrotfish *Chlorurus gibbus*

Size: to 70cm

The Red Sea population differs in colour from the rest of the Indo-Pacific. Common. Previously in Genus *Scarus*.

Rüppell, 1829

Terminal male

Initial phase

Bullethead Parrotfish *Chlorurus sordidus*

Size: to 40m

Initial phase

Terminal male

Common at all levels. Young fish are usually seen in schools. The white area containing the black spot on the caudal base can be quickly turned on and off. Previously in the Genus *Scarus*.

Forsskål, 1775

Longnose Parrotfish *Hipposcarus harid*

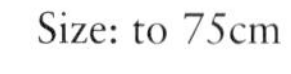

Size: to 75cm

Terminal male

Initial phase

Night colours

Quite common, especially on the first shelf. Sometimes seen in large schools.

Forsskål, 1775

Seagrass Parrotfish *Leptoscarus vaigiensis*

Size: to 35cm

Usually found in seagrass beds, occasionally over areas of abundant algae. Photograph shows male and female.

Quoy & Gaimard, 1825

Rusty Parrotfish *Scarus ferrugineus*

Size: to 40cm

Initial phase

Terminal male

Red Sea to Gulf of Oman. Very common at all levels.

Forsskål, 1775

Bridled Parrotfish *Scarus frenatus*

Size: to 45cm

Initial phase

Terminal male

Common at all levels.

Lacepède, 1802

Purplebrown Parrotfish *Scarus fuscopurpureus*

Size: to 38cm

Found in the Red Sea and Arabian Gulf. Initial phase greenish brown with three indistinct wide bands on body; a hint of purple at back of dorsal fin and on the tail fin.

Klunzinger, 1871

Bluebarred Parrotfish *Scarus ghobban*

Size: to 75cm

Common in north Red Sea, less so in central area. Initial phase similar but with prominent blue bands on head, more blue colour on scales, and lacking tail extensions.

Forsskål, 1775

Parrotfish are not easy to approach - they are always on the move, and are all wary fish.

There are believed to be 19 species of Parrotfish in the Red Sea, although at times this ubiquitous fish appears to have many more cousins! The most abundant appears to be the Bullethead, particularly in its young adult colouration.

In the southern Farasan islands of the Red Sea an annual festival is prompted by the mass swarming of Longnose Parrotfish *(Hipposcarus harid)* in the shallow water of a particular bay in the islands. This phenomenon is as yet unexplained - it provides a bumper fish catch for all the local residents, but unfortunately the coral is badly damaged in the process of catching the fish.

Parrotfishes (Scaridae)

Bolbometopon	*muricatum*	*Scarus*	*collana*[1]
Calotomus	*viridescens*[1]	*Scarus*	*ferrugineus*
Cetoscarus	*bicolor*	*Scarus*	*frenatus*
Chlorurus	*genazonatus*[1]	*Scarus*	*fuscopurpureus*
Chlorurus	*gibbus*	*Scarus*	*ghobban*
Chlorurus	*sordidus*	*Scarus*	*niger*
Hipposcarus	*harid*	*Scarus*	*psittacus*
Leptoscarus	*vaigiensis*	*Scarus*	*rubroviolaceus*[2]
		Scarus	*viridifucatus*[2]

1 Red Sea species 2 Red Sea

Notes on Juvenile Parrotfishes

There is very little information available to help identify juvenile Parrotfishes. If a small, unfamiliar striped fish is found, either in the shallows or down to the first shelf, the chances are that it is a Parrotfish. To help identify these fish, some of which may transition through different colour forms, brief descriptions are given below. Most of these descriptions result from the authors' observations - photographs of 4 young Parrotfish, which have not been identified, are also included, and can be assumed to be one of the undescribed species.

Bolbometopon muricatum **Bumphead Parrotfish**
Brown with 2 longitudinal rows of whitish spots on top of body.

Cetoscarus bicolor **Bicolour Parrotfish**
White/light brown orange. Orange edged black spot on dorsal.

Hipposcarus harid **Longnose Parrotfish**
Light tan dorsally, shading on sides and ventrally, to greenish/white, with a narrow white band containing a blackish spot at base of caudal fin.

Swarthy Parrotfish *Scarus niger*

Size: to 40cm

Initial phase **Terminal male**

Common; the male is readily identified by the bright yellow mark above the pectoral fin.

Forsskål, 1775

Palenose Parrotfish *Scarus psittacus*

Size: to 25cm

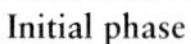

Initial phase **Terminal male**

A small species, common at all levels.

Forsskål, 1775

Juvenile Parrotfishes

Bicolour Parrotfish

Rusty Parrotfish

Scarus ferrugineus **Rusty Parrotfish**
Yellow tail, brown with pale bluish abdomen, two white longitudinal stripes, one mouth to caudal, other snout to caudal. Next stage loses stripes, retains light blue belly.

Scarus frenatus **Bridled Parrotfish**
Reddish brown at front, shading to greenish white at tail. Red on dorsal fin. Broad dark band, snout to eye.

Scarus ghobban **Bluebarred Parrotfish**
Tan stripes, paler interspaces. Belly off-white, fins orange/yellow.

Chlorurus gibbus **Steepheaded Parrotfish**
Olive/black, with three horizontal white stripes.

Scarus niger **Swarthy Parrotfish**
Blue/brown with rows of small light blue spots - caudal fin white, with black spot on top and below base.

Scarus psittacus **Palenose Parrotfish**
Reddish/Brown with black spot on pectoral base, and dark spot on first dorsal. Paler coloured nose. Abruptly pale off-white below pectoral base.

Chlorurus sordidus **Bullethead Parrotfish**
Four black lines (broadest through the eye) on white (or yellow) background - next stage, white cauduncle with black spot.

Scarus rubroviolaceus **Ember Parrotfish**
Bright pale yellow with three dark lines (broadest through the eye). Four whitish bands, prominent on dorsal and anal fin rays. White dots on caudal fin.

Rabbitfishes

Rabbitfish are very common in the shallow areas along coastlines. They are popular eating fishes amongst local people, and very easy to catch. They should, however, be handled very carefully since their fin spines have poison glands associated with them that can inflict a very painful wound.

Rabbitfishes are allied to Surgeonfishes, are of the same basic shape, and will often be seen in the company of Surgeonfishes. The most notable difference is that most species lack the bright colours of most Surgeonfish and they have a greater number of anal fin spines. Like Surgeonfishes, they are roving grazers of algae and vegetable matter. There are 4 species reported in the Red Sea, whereas the Indian Ocean contains some 25 species.

Juvenile Parrotfishes

Bridled Parrotfish

Swarthy Parrotfish

Bullethead Parrotfish

Ember Parrotfish

Unidentified Juveniles

Perhaps the only exception to the otherwise rather dull coloured Rabbitfishes is the Stellate which will often be seen, usually in pairs or small groups under the fringing reef. They are cautious fish and slow moving and form a rather elegant contribution to the reef fauna.

When alarmed, the small silvery Rabbitfish in the shallow areas will form a very tight formation, with individuals so close together that the formation could be mistaken for a single large silver fish - perhaps a very clever deception to deter predators.

Rabbitfishes can perform very quick colour changes when threatened or alarmed - they can assume a mottled/blotchy skin pattern to blend better with their environment. At night (they are diurnal) they adopt this mottled appearance when they sleep in coral crevices or rubble. A Rabbitfish will sometimes when alarmed 'flutter' its dorsal fin.

Rabbitfishes (Siganidae)

Siganus	*argenteus*	*Siganus*	*rivulatus*[1]
Siganus	*luridus*	*Siganus*	*stellatus laqueus*[2]

1 Red Sea species 2 Red Sea sub-species of *S. stellatus*

Remoras

Remoras are not strictly reef fishes. The various species (3 in the Red Sea) are, however, sometimes associated with reef fishes, in particular the large Wrasses and Parrotfishes.

Remoras present one of the most common forms of commensalism, that close association between two animals that is beneficial to only one of the partners.

The only species that is likely to be encountered by divers close to the reef is the Sharksucker, which sometimes swims alone, possibly searching for a new host.

The usual diet of these fish is composed of scraps lost or discarded by a large host animal, which could be a Shark, Ray or Turtle. Sharksuckers attach themselves by means of their adapted dorsal fins, which have evolved into suckers - this attachment is so light that it can hardly be felt by the host. We have twice played host to one of these fascinating fish - once off Port Sudan when a passing Manta Ray donated one of its camp followers to me, and more recently whilst diving with my c0-author off the fringing reef near Jeddah, when an apparently lost individual kept our company throughout our dive, attaching itself occasionally to one of us.

Remora (Echeneidae)

Remorina	*albescens*
Echeneis	*naucrates*

Forktail Rabbitfish *Siganus argenteus*

Size: to 37cm

Solitary or in small aggregations, usually in shallow water.

Quoy and Gaimard, 1825

Squaretail Rabbitfish *Siganus luridus*

Size: to 25cm

Often solitary; photo shows dark phase.

Cuvier, 1829

Rivulated Rabbitfish *Siganus rivulatus*

Size: to 30cm

Also known as Red Sea Rabbitfish. Very common especially in shallow water; rapidly changes from uniform grey to mottled brown when alarmed or hiding. Sometimes in large schools.

Forsskål, 1775

Sandperches

There are three genera of Sandperches (also called Grubfishes) but only one occurs in the Red Sea, represented by three species. The only species likely to be encountered in the reef environment is the Spotted Sandperch, which is numerous in sandy areas.

Characteristically it will be found on the bottom, propped up by its pelvic fins - it is an overall beige colour, with a row of black, yellow edged, spots above its long anal fin.

The head markings identify the sex of the species - in males the head is marked by lines, in females by spots.

Sandperches are approachable, and will only move away at the last minute - they are carnivorous and their habits are similar to those of the Lizardfishes.

They are opportunistic, and will keep a close eye on the activities of Goatfish, darting in when a tasty morsal is revealed.

Sandperches (Pinguipedidae)
Parapercis hexophthalma`

Sanddivers (Trichonotidae)
Trichonotus nikii

Snappers, Grunts & Spinecheeks

Of approximately 300 species of Snapper found worldwide only about 32 are reported as Red Sea inhabitants. They are one of the most important food fishes, and some of the species can grow to very large size.

Like many of the favoured food fishes, the larger members of the Snapper family are not often seen along the Jeddah area coastline. When seen, however, a large school of Black and White Snappers can be quite an intimidating sight. They congregate in large shoals during the day in open water, motionless with eyes grimly staring, their upward slanting mouths giving them a funereal appearance. This rather dull, untidy looking fish develops from one of the most striking of juveniles which is usually seen on its own over deep water against the reef. The juvenile sports a striking black and white body pattern which can be seen from many metres away.

The origin of the name Snapper is usually attributed to the habit of some of the species of convulsively snapping their jaws.

The largest Snapper to be seen in the Red Sea is the Twinspot, more commonly known by its arabic name Bohar. Large adult Bohar are solitary fish, difficult to approach, and will be seen over deep water close to the reef. The juvenile Bohar, which bears the two white body spots which give this species its name, will be seen swimming rapidly amongst coral outcrops, where, apart from the white markings, it could be mistaken for a large Ternate Chromis, with its shiny brown appearance. They also appear to shoal with Scissor-tail Sergeant Damselfishes.

Stellate Rabbitfish *Siganus stellatus laqueus*

Size: to 35cm

Almost always in pairs; Red Sea individuals have a slightly different distribution of spots compared to those from the Indo Pacific.

Forsskål, 1775

Sharksucker *Echeneis naucrates*

Size: to 90cm

Adult (max size)

On author's arm

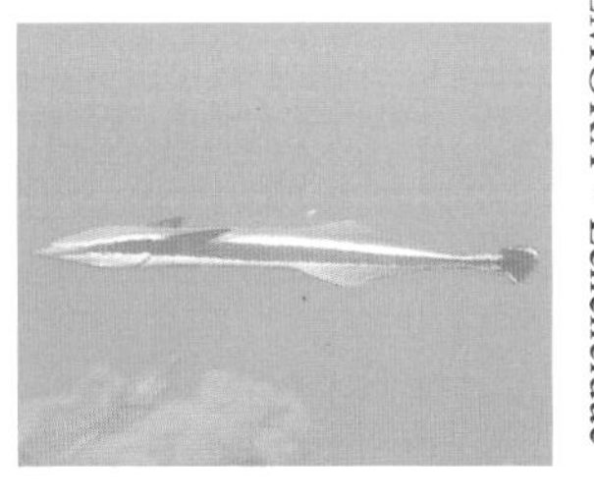

Most commonly associated with sharks, but also often with turtles and the larger species of reef fishes; sometimes free living. The pair pictured are probably maximum size, and were seen soon after a large Manta Ray was reported in the vicinity.

Linnaeus, 1758

Spotted Sandperch *Parapercis hexophthalma*

Size: to 23cm

Female

Male

Very common on first shelf, usually sitting motionless on sand or a small rock.

Cuvier, 1829

On the whole, Snappers are shy fish - however the pretty Bluestripe Snapper is an exception, which I have known to follow a diver, trying to catch air bubbles.

A number of the Snappers are deep-water fish and will not be seen by amateur divers. These fishes are not found in water less than 80m. They are all a light shade of red, varying from pink to crimson, and all are commonly known as Red Snappers. They are excellent food fish, and are therefore more likely to be seen in the fish market than the water. Included in this group are species of the genus Etelis, Pristipomoides, Aprion and Argyrops.

Grunts are similar to Snappers in appearance and habits. They differ in having smaller mouths with the top lip projecting (Snappers generally have a slightly projecting lower jaw). The lips of Grunts are fleshy (hence the alternative name of Sweetlips). The name Grunt is derived from the fish's ability to make sound by grinding its teeth.

Grunts are essentially nocturnal and rather cautious fish. They stay close to the reef by day, often in small schools; the most frequently seen of the Grunts, because of its strong black on yellow colouring perhaps, is the Blackspotted Grunt.

Juvenile Grunts tend to be quite dissimilar in colour and form to adults, which leads to some confusion in identification. Juveniles are also reported to secrete a toxic skin mucus, to dissuade predators.

Spinecheeks (Snapper relatives) are represented in the Red Sea by 9 species, but only one, the Dotted Spinecheek is likely to be seen, since the others are mostly deeper water fishes.

The Dotted Spinecheek will always be present around the fringing reef, and sandy areas below it. It is easily recognised by its bright silvery body, the top part of which is dark with yellowish silver longitudinal lines. The most striking feature is perhaps its large eyes with two broad yellow bars through them, following the body line markings.

The Spinecheek derives its name from the presence of a short backward pointing spine below the eye. It is not a very active fish, and is often solitary.

At least one author has reported the presence of two other Spinecheeks, Scolopsis taeniata and Scolopsis bimaculatus, to be within amateur diving depth in the Red Sea.

Snappers (Lutjanidae)

Aprion	*virescens*	*Lutjanus*	*kasmira*
Lutjanus	*argentimaculatus*	*Lutjanus*	*lutjanus*
Lutjanus	*bengalensis*	*Lutjanus*	*monostigma*
Lutjanus	*bohar*	*Lutjanus*	*rivulatus*
Lutjanus	*caeruleolineatus* [1]	*Lutjanus*	*russelli*
Lutjanus	*ehrenbergii*	*Lutjanus*	*sanguineus*
Lutjanus	*fulviflammus*	*Lutjanus*	*sebae*
Lutjanus	*fulvus*	*Macolor*	*niger*
Lutjanus	*gibbus*	*Paracaesio*	*sordida*
Lutjanus	*johnii*	*Pinjalo*	*pinjalo*

Mangrove Jack *Lutjanus argentimaculatus*

Size: to 80cm

Seen over deep drop-offs, often in small groups.

Forsskål, 1775

Twinspot Snapper *Lutjanus bohar*

Size: to 100cm

A solitary species, very often seen over deep water off the fringing reef.

Forsskål, 1775

Juvenile

Blackspot Snapper *Lutjanus ehrenbergii*

Size: to 30cm

The small photograph shows the juvenile.

Peters, 1869

Dory Snapper *Lutjanus fulviflammus*

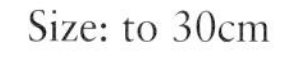

Size: to 30cm

Usually solitary, sometimes in pairs. Adults have black spot on lateral line.

Forsskål, 1775

Humpback Snapper *Lutjanus gibbus*

Size: to 60cm

Not often seen. Hides in coral caverns.

Forsskål, 1775

Bluestripe Snapper *Lutjanus kasmira*

Size: to 34cm

Common in groups, sometimes containing a large number. They make a colourful contribution to the reef scene. This large group was photographed in a wreck.

Forsskål, 1775

Onespot Snapper *Lutjanus monostigma*

Size: to 60cm

Older individuals lose their black spot.

Cuvier, 1828

Black and White Snapper *Macolor niger*

Size: to 60cm

Young are solitary, and difficult to approach. Adults usually form large schools.

Forsskål, 1775

Juvenile

Blackspotted Grunt *Plectorhinchus gaterinus*

Size: to 45cm

Quite common in reef faces, and also in wreckage areas.

Forsskål, 1775

Juvenile

Harraway's Grunt *Plectorhinchus harrawayi*

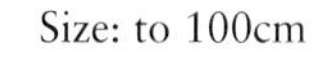

Size: to 100cm

Usually paired - not common.

Smith, 1952

Painted Grunt *Diagramma pictum*

Size: to 90cm

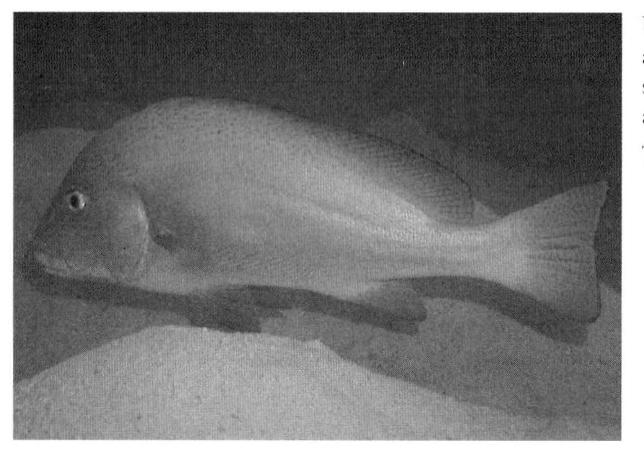

Usually found in silty reef areas. During the day it may be stationary above the bottom, and easily approachable.

Thunberg, 1792

Dotted Spinecheek *Scolopsis ghanam*

Size: to 20cm

Usually solitary and inactive. Sometimes forms large groups.

Forsskål, 1775

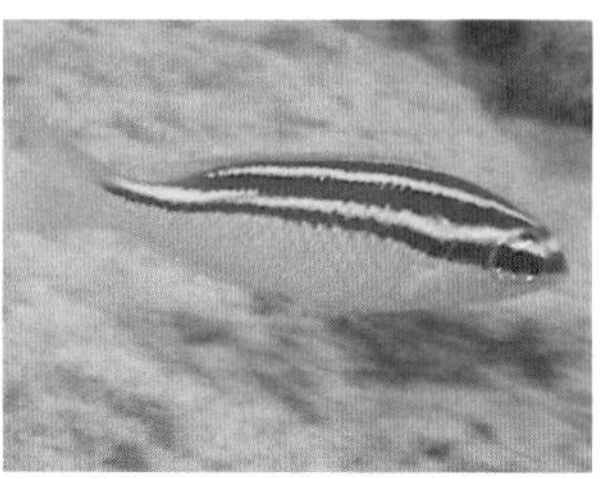

Juvenile

Grunts (Haemulidae)			
Plectorhinchus	*flavomaculatus*[2]	*Plectorhinchus*	*schotaf*
Plectorhinchus	*gaterinus*	*Plectorhinchus*	*sordidus*
Plectorhinchus	*gibbosus*[2]	*Plectorhinchus*	*playfairi*[2]
Plectorhinchus	*harrawayi*	*Pomadasys*	*furcatus*[2]
Diagramma	*pictum*	*Pomadasys*	*opercularis*

Spinecheeks (Nemipteridae)			
Scolopsis	*bimaculatus*	*Scolopsis*	*taeniatus*
Scolopsis	*ghanam*	*Scolopsis*	*vosmeri*

1 Red Sea species 2 Southern Red Sea only

Spadefishes

There are four species of Spadefish (or Batfish) in the genus Platax, three of which may be encountered, usually in small groups, in the Red Sea. They are unmistakable by genus, but sometimes difficult to identify by species. Generally they are very deep-bodied, small-mouthed fishes, silver based with at least two broad dark bands, one of which crosses the eye.

Individual species change their shape significantly with age - as a juvenile, the Circular Spadefish *(P. orbicularis)* can be unrecognisable as a fish - it resembles a small red/brown leaf fluttering through the water. The Pinnate Spadefish *(P. pinnatus)* juvenile has the colour of a common black bodied, yellow/orange edged nudibranch, which is known to be distasteful to predator fishes.

Spadefishes are diurnal and feed on zooplankton, small invertebrates, worms and jellyfish.

Large specimens of Spadefish can be found in very shallow water, under piers and other man-made structures - they appear to enjoy murky water and the less scenic areas of reef.

In the open water they seem attracted to the shady underside of boats.

Spadefishes (Ephippidae)			
Platax	*pinnatus*[1]	*Platax*	*teira*
Platax	*orbicularis*		

1 NB Although listed as a Red Sea resident, there is some doubt of its presence. It is known from the Pacific region.

Circular Spadefish *Platax orbicularis*

Size: to 40cm

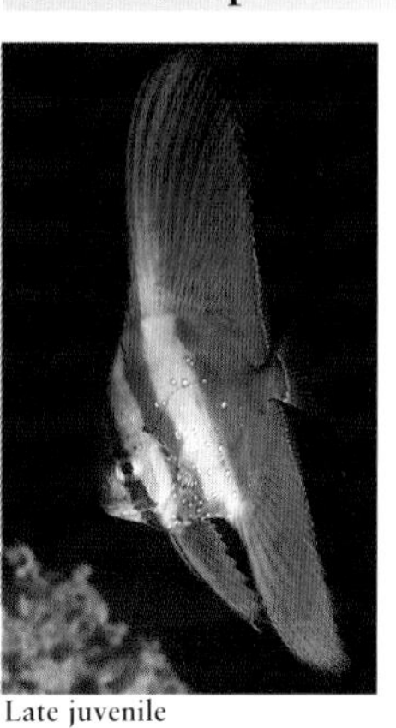

Late juvenile

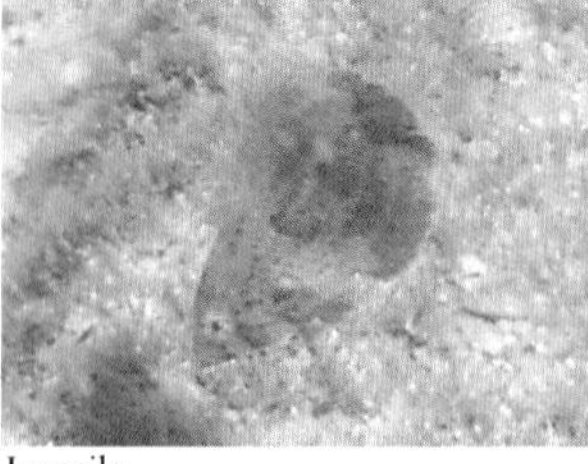

Juvenile

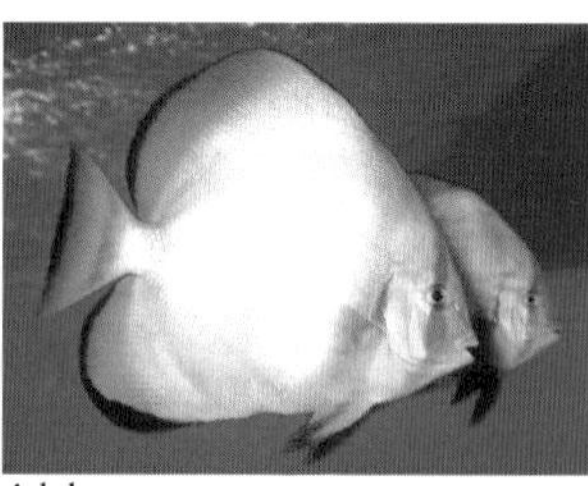

Adult

Spadefish will often be found under man-made structures. Juveniles appear to casual observers as a piece of detritus (sometimes described as a leaf) fluttering in the water.

Forsskål, 1775

Black Surgeonfish *Acanthurus nigricans*

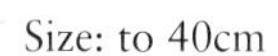

Size: to 40cm

Red Sea to Arabian Gulf. Sometimes seen in small groups. Prefers the open water.

Linnaeus, 1758

Brown Surgeonfish *Acanthurus nigrofuscus*

Size: to 20cm

Common in all areas near the reef.

Forsskål, 1775

Surgeonfishes & Unicornfishes

Surgeonfishes are abundant in the Red Sea and will be seen in the shallows, on the top and side of the reef and at the base. The first-time snorkeller swimming on the top of the fringing reef may experience his first moments of anxiety when confronted with a large, strikingly coloured, Sohal. These fish maintain a strict dominance on the fringing reef top, and will readily challenge a swimmer, who will be well advised to move away. A Surgeonfish is capable of inflicting a deep wound, by sweeping its tail towards a threat - its tail boasts at its base very sharp knife edge spines. This action is defensive, but will appear to swimmers as very aggressive.

These spines at the base of the tail, on both sides, give the Surgeonfishes their common family name. Usually the spines are centred in a very brightly coloured area, thereby informing other fish of the presence of this armament.

The spines on the Surgeonfish are hinged at the base, and will extend as the fish curves its body - it appears to be a purely mechanical action, not controlled by the brain.

Surgeonfishes feed on algae and zooplankton and are often to be seen grazing rocks and coral - their low, small mouth is well suited to this practice.

Of the 17 reported Surgeonfishes seen in the Red Sea, the Sailfin perhaps provides the most elegant example. As a juvenile it could be mistaken for a small angelfish, with its oversize dorsal and anal fins, and brightly coloured yellow body with black markings. Although the young Sailfin loses the yellow, it does become an elaborately marked, and impressive, adult.

Unicornfishes are endowed with similar defence equipment to the Surgeonfishes, though these fish have fixed, unhinged, hard blades at the base of their tails. They also have brightly coloured areas around their spines - the spines of the Bluespine Unicornfish show well when the fish is viewed from above as bright splashes of colour. Some Unicornfishes have more than one spine, whilst others have just a small hard projection instead of a spine.

Unicornfishes tend to be observed over deeper water - the largest (which does not, however, sport the protruding horn characteristic of the family) is the Sleek Unicornfish, which is often seen in shoals.

Some species of Unicornfish will occasionally enter very shallow water in search of algae patches - if frightened, they will quickly disappear into a hole, in much the same way as a Triggerfish.

The forward protuberance of the Spotted and the Bluespine Unicornfish appears to develop with age - the purpose of this device is unclear. A well-endowed Unicornfish, as an algae and zooplankton feeder, must find such a protuberance decidely inconvenient.

The Orangespine and Bluespine varieties develop long streamers from the top and bottom of the tail as they grow old.

Sohal Surgeonfish *Acanthurus sohal*

Size: to 40cm

Red Sea and Arabian Gulf. Very common on reef tops and sides. Sometimes threatening.

Forsskål, 1775

Juvenile

Lined Bristletooth Surgeonfish *Ctenochaetus striatus*

Size: to 25cm

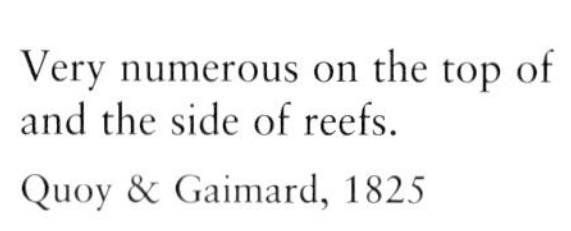

Very numerous on the top of and the side of reefs.

Quoy & Gaimard, 1825

Juvenile

Sailfin Surgeonfish *Zebrasoma veliferum*

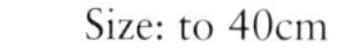

Size: to 40cm

Usually seen in pairs, but large groups have been reported. Individuals freely mix with other Surgeonfish species.

Bloch, 1795

Juvenile

Yellowtail Surgeonfish *Zebrasoma xanthurum*

Size: to 20cm

Red Sea and Arabian Gulf. Found singly or in pairs. They are reported to form large schools in the Gulf, but this has not been observed in the Red Sea by the authors.

Blyth, 1852

Spotted Unicornfish *Naso brevirostris*

Size: to 60cm

Found in small groups at the edge of reefs and at drop-offs. Horn develops with age. Juveniles found on top of reefs.

Valenciennes, 1835

Sleek Unicornfish *Naso hexacanthus*

Size: to 75cm

Found in small groups in open water by the reef.
Large individuals sometimes solitary. Can assume all over light blue/white colour.

Bleeker, 1855

Surgeonfish (Acanthuridae)

Acanthurus	*bleekeri*[2]		
Acanthurus	*sohal*[1]	*Ctenochaetus*	*striatus*
Acanthurus	*nigricans*[1]	*Zebrasoma*	*veliferum*
Acanthurus	*nigrofuscus*	*Zebrasoma*	*xanthurum*[1]

Unicornfish (Acanthuridae)

Naso	*brevirostris*	*Naso*	*hexacanthus*
Naso	*lituratus*	*Naso*	*unicornis*

1 Red Sea species
2 *Acanthurus bleekeri* is reported only from the southern Red Sea

NB. Surgeonfishes (known also as Tangs) and Unicornfish are classified in separate subfamilies (Acanthurinae and Nasinae) of the family Acanthuridae.

Sweepers

Sweepers are ever present in reef faces, seldom venturing farther than a metre from the security of the reef. Two species are common in the Red Sea - the Vanikoro Sweeper *(Pempheris vanicolensis)*, and its smaller relative, *Parapriacanthus ransonneti* which is commonly known as Glassfish (a name that should be reserved for a family of small fishes in the Ambassidae family). The latter form very dense schools in caves and dark overhangs, and when light is directed on them they reflect a bright yellow tinged silver.

The Copper Sweeper, *P. oualensis*, is less often seen - it appears very similar to the Vanikoro, but lacks the black margin on the anal fin.

The Sweeper is known in some parts of the world as the Helicopter fish - readers who are familiar with the shape of helicopters of the 1950s will appreciate the analogy. The Pempheris Sweepers are shiny bronze in colour, have very large eyes, and a sharply oblique mouth.

Sweeper (Pempheridae)

Pempheris	*vanicolensis*	*Parapriacanthus*	*ransonneti*
Pempheris	*oualensis*		

Tilefishes

The two species of Tilefish most commonly seen in the Red Sea are the Striped Blanquillo and the Quakerfish. These are two of only three known species in the Sea. Both may be observed at the first shelf level, over a sandy or rubble bottom.

Orangespine Unicornfish *Naso lituratus*

Size: to 25cm

Very numerous around reefs.

Bloch & Schneider, 1801

Juvenile

Bluespine Unicornfish *Naso unicornis*

Size: to 70cm

Small individuals can be seen on the top and sides of reefs. As they grow, they migrate to deeper water. They develop a small horn and extended caudal tail filaments as they mature.

Forsskål, 1775

Golden Sweeper *Parapriacanthus ransonneti*

Size: to 8cm

Nocturnal, during the day found in large aggregations in caves and large crevices. Previously known as *P. guentheri*

Steindachner, 1870

Vanikoro Sweeper *Pempheris vanicolensis*

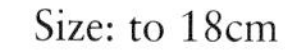

Size: to 18cm

Seen in large groups in gaps in the reef.

Cuvier, 1831

Quakerfish *Malacanthus brevirostris*

Size: to 32cm

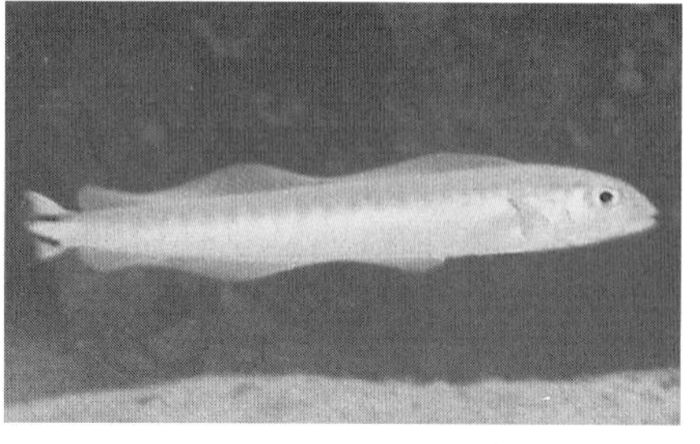

Most likely to be seen, in pairs, on the first shelf. Stays very close to the sandy bottom. Additional photo shows an individual with unusual markings, photographed in the north Red Sea.

Guichenot, 1848

Striped Blanquillo *Malacanthus latovittatus*

Size: to 43cm

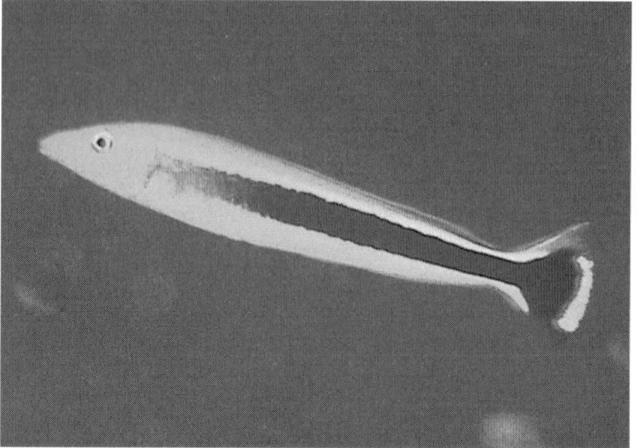

Invariably in pairs, usually on first shelf, hovering over the sand.

Lacepède, 1801

The Striped Blanquillo is a very wary fish that tends to keep its distance from divers. It has the shape of a cigar Wrasse, although it is a very much larger fish. It has a distinct colouration, unusual in fishes, being an overall pale silvery blue. It has a dark stripe along its lateral line, which terminates at the base of the caudal fin, giving way to a distinctively marked tail, of a silver/white background with striking black markings. Blanquillo are very often seen in pairs. They will be observed hovering about 1m above the sand looking for food, and will make a sudden dive to snatch a small crustacean or other small creature.

The Quakerfish is much smaller than the Blanquillo and just as wary of humans. It is overall grey in colour, with two distinct horizontal black lines on its tail. It lives in burrows, much like members of the Goby family.

Tilefishes (Malacanthidae)
Hoplolatilus oreni *Malacanthus brevirostris*
Malacanthus latovittatus

Wrasses

The Wrasses form the family Labridae which contains at least 300 species (some authors claim 500-600), 72 of which are reported to live in the Red Sea. They are found in most seas, but are most numerous around coral reefs in shallow tropical seas.

Although they come in many shapes and sizes, they may generally be classified as elongate, with long dorsal and anal fins, and some may attain 2m in length.The colour variations of many Wrasses can confuse the amateur identifier - colours, and their patterns, change according to age and sex.

They are generally omnivorous although they principally feed on marine invertebrates.

Some small, or young, Wrasses feed on the external parasites of larger fish - such activity provides protection for young Wrasses as well as a source of food.

Wrasses are on the whole solitary fish, and do not stray far from their chosen areas of reef. However, some of the smaller species (such as the Eightline Wrasse) will form large groups, which when studied will be found to contain dominant males with their female harems. These smaller Wrasses in large schools are plankton feeders, and form a colourful complement to the reef face.

Wrasses are very active fish - their elongate shape and oily scales allow them to move swiftly. Many are characterised by their swimming movement which is jerky as a result of swimming mainly with their pectoral fins. Viewed from above, their swimming action is somewhat comic. The energy expended in their daily pursuits may account for their long sleeping period. Wrasses are active in daylight and enjoy a long, early sleep - many bury themselves in sand or coral gravel, appearing only when the day is long started for most diurnal fish.

The courtship and breeding behaviour of a number of Wrasses is notable. Males will dance and cavort before its mate, and when both are ready, they will rise vertically ejecting eggs and sperm at a synchonised moment. This action has been witnessed by the authors in a home aquarium, and the occasion provided a gourmet diversion for the other residents. During the courtship, the male may change colour and pattern very rapidly in his excitement.

Perhaps the best known, and best loved of all the Wrasses is the brave little Cleaner Wrasse. The Cleaner will maintain its own cleaning station, and be available to all who may require a general service. Since parasites are its principal food, and they occur not only on the host fishes exterior but also within the mouth and gills, a complete service can be a hazardous experience for the Cleaner. If the Cleaner is unsure of the willingness of a host to allow him to remove parasites, it will perform an elaborate dance which appears to seduce the host fish into submission.

Whilst some mature Wrasses may be only 5cm in length, the family Labridae contains a very large member, the Humphead, or Napolean Wrasse, which may weigh over 100kg. The Humphead in maturity is a popular photographic subject, and is quite tame when approached under water in popular diving areas.

There are other Wrasses which do not conform in shape or habits to the stereotype. Of note in the Red Sea, the Slingjaw Wrasse (a favourite of the authors) may easily be mistaken for a Grouper when in its intermediate stage of development. The Slingjaw juvenile is a very wary fish and is seldom seen. Coloured orange/brown with three bands of white dots on a black background, and five similar bands radiating from the eye, it becomes all brown until it reaches its first mature stage, which is female, when it becomes a bright yellow. Thereafter she may change sex, depending on the local male/female population, to the multi coloured male with white head, black eyestreak and orange forehead. The mature female will often be observed as overall grey, with suggestions of the male markings. The juvenile Slingjaw can be mistaken for the adult Wetmorella nigropinnata, which, like the juvenile Slingjaw, favours the back dark corners of caves and is difficult to see clearly.

The Slingjaw is named for its extendable jaw, which performs the action of a vacuum cleaner on unfortunate small crustaceans and invertebrates.

Although the authors are unaware of any strict symbiotic relationships of Wrasses, apart from the cleaning relationship, he has observed on several occasions young Wrasses, notably Moon Wrasses, hiding amongst tentacles of anemones, in company with young two bar anemone fish - whether these young fish gain temporary immunity from the sting of the anemone, or simply avoid being stung, is difficult to judge.

On a number of occasions, the authors have observed an Orangespotted Jack in very close company with a male Slingjaw Wrasse, of similar size. It seemed an unlikely relationship, since the two fish have such different behavioural characteristics - other authors have recorded that Jacks will sometimes shadow, or 'ride', other fishes in order to get near to prey. The Slingjaw Wrasse is reported by

Bluespotted Wrasse *Anampses caeruleopunctatus*

Size: to 40cm

Female shown. Not often seen, uncommon. The male is blue/green with a broad green band between the eyes and narrow irregular blue bands on head and fins.

Rüppell, 1829

Yellowtail Wrasse *Anampses meleagrides*

Size: to 21cm

Not very common. Female much more noticeable, with her prominent colours. Males dull brown with vertical blue lines on scales and irregular blue lines on head. Tail orangish with a white crescent.

Valenciennes, 1839

Yellowbreasted Wrasse *Anampses twistii*

Size: to 18cm

Common along the first shelf - they seem to prefer coral outcrops on sand.

Bleeker, 1856

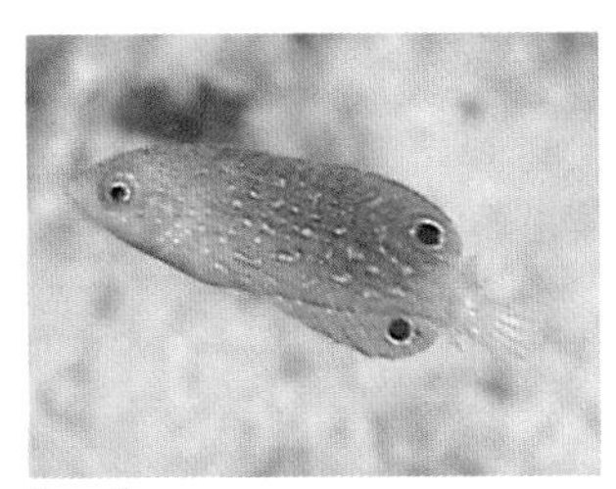

Juvenile

Adult

Ormond to 'associate' with certain other non Wrasse species, using its ability to change colour to mix with them - notably with Brown Surgeonfishes. Ormond also noted that in it's yellow form, the Slingjaw may associate with Sulphur Damselfishes and the Masked Butterflyfishes, both of which are bright yellow.

A very common 'association' involving Wrasses is that of the Mental Wrasse and either the Forsskål's Goatfish or the Long-barbel Goatfish - the Wrasse may be seen very close to a Goatfish, whilst adopting a very convincing disguise, matching the Goatfish's colour pattern very closely.

The Bandcheek Wrasse will also sometimes be seen imitating Goatfish.

Divers will notice the tendency of both the Bandcheek and the Mental Wrasses to approach them. The Bandcheek can appear quite menacing, with its projecting lower jaw usually showing a fine set of teeth. They are well built fishes, but do not grow to much more than 25cm. The Mental Wrasse (named we assume for its large chin, and not for the colloquial meaning of mental - although sometimes I think the latter fits better!) will approach a diver with a distinctly unfriendly look in its eye.

Many of the Wrasses are opportunists - the Checkerboard Wrasse will often be seen amongst Goatfish stealing small crustaceans revealed by the Goatfish barbels. A diver stirring the silt or sand will soon attract Wrasses keen for a free meal. Certainly the Redbreasted Wrasse will always be near disturbed sand whether caused by Goatfish or careless divers.

An activity often seen between fishes of the same species and sex, and Wrasses in particular, is a form of apparent mouth-to-mouth confrontation, which appears to be a friendly, but may in fact be a warning process. Some authors claim that this activity is part of courtship, but since I have observed two females (and also two juvenile Parrotfishes) behaving in this manner I have some doubts. I have read of no other explanation for this behaviour.

Wrasses of the *Hemigymnus* genus are characterised by large fleshy lips. The two species that will be seen in the Red Sea, the Barred Wrasse and the Thicklip Wrasse, exhibit an ability to reverse colours. Debelius notes that the Barred Wrasse can reverse the colour of its vertical bands, and the author has observed two large Thicklips together, one with the forward part of the body paler than the rear, and the other paler at the rear.

The three species in the genus *Bodianus* are commonly known as Hogfishes. All three are attractively marked species; the *B.axillaris* (Axilspot) juvenile is very striking with its large white spots on a totally black body - as it grows into the initial phase (female) it retains the white spots, but its body colour becomes a deep brown and its fins are tinted with bright orange.

Wrasses (Labridae)

Anampses	*caeruleopunctatus*	*Hemigymnus*	*fasciatus*
Anampses	*lineatus*	*Hemigymnus*	*melapterus*
Anampses	*meleagrides*	*Hologymnosus*	*annulatus*

Genus	Species
Anampses	*twistii*
Bodianus	*axillaris*
Bodianus	*diana*
Bodianus	*anthioides*
Cheilinus	*abudjubbe*[1]
Cheilinus	*lunulatus*[1]
Cheilinus	*undulatus*
Cheilinus	*fasciatus*
Cheilio	*inermis*
Choerodon	*robustus*
Cirrhilabrus	*blatteus*[1,2]
Cirrhilabrus	*rubriventralis*[1,2]
Coris	*africana*
Coris	*aygula*
Coris	*variegata*
Coris	*caudimacula*
Epibulus	*insidiator*
Gomphosus	*caeruleus klunzingeri*[1]
Halichoeres	*hortulanus*
Halichoeres	*marginatus*
Halichoeres	*nebulosus*
Halichoeres	*scapularis*
Halichoeres	*zeylonicus*
Labroides	*dimidiatus*
Larabicus	*quadrilineatus*[1]
Macropharyngodon	*biparitus marisrubri*[1]
Minilabrus	*striatus*[1]
Novaculichthys	*macrolepidotus*
Novaculichthys	*taeniourus*
Oxycheilinus	*digrammus*
Oxycheilinus	*mentalis*
Paracheilinus	*octotaenia*[1]
Pseudocheilinus	*evanidus*
Pseudocheilinus	*hexataenia*
Pseudodax	*moluccanus*
Pteragogus	*cryptus*
Stethojulis	*albovittata*
Stethojulis	*interrupta*
Thalassoma	*klunzingeri*[1]
Thalassoma	*lunare*
Thalassoma	*purpureum*
Wetmorella	*nigropinnata*
Xyrichtys	*pavo*
Xyrichtys	*bimaculatus*
Xyrichtys	*pentadactylus*

1 Red Sea species

2 The two Social Wrasses, members of the genus *Cirrhilabrus*, are reported only from the northern Red Sea, and are quite rare. *C. blatteus* is found below 40m.

Flounders & Soles

Although these fishes are not strictly reef fishes, they are included since they are very common in shallow sandy areas where they will be seen by snorkellers. They are excellently camouflaged, to the extent of being almost invisible; they adapt their colouration and pattern according to their surroundings, so that they can barely be distinguished. They will often also have a light covering of sand over their bodies.

Flounders and Soles are similar, except for the location of their eyes. Both have both eyes on one side of the head, the Flounders' on the left side and the Soles' on the right side.

In the larval stage the eyes are on opposite sides of the head, and as the fish develops the eyes migrate to one side.

Abudjubbe Wrasse *Cheilinus abudjubbe*

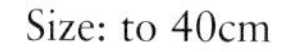

Size: to 40cm

Adult male

Red Sea only, common and solitary. Often seen in the lagoon areas, close to the fringing reef.

Rüppell, 1835

Juvenile

Redbreasted Wrasse *Cheilinus fasciatus*

Size: to 35cm

Adult

Solitary and common on the first shelf. Follows schools of Goatfish. Unafraid of divers.

Bloch, 1791

Juvenile

Broomtail Wrasse *Cheilinus lunulatus*

Size: to 50cm

Male

Red Sea and Arabian Gulf. Solitary and difficult to approach. Colours can be quite striking.

Forsskål, 1775

Female

Humphead Wrasse *Cheilinus undulatus* (Napoleon Wrasse Size: to 230cm

Solitary or in small groups. The largest Wrasse, which can become used to divers and be approachable. The author has observed a group of 8 of them associated with a single Bumphead Parrotfish. (Rüppell, 1835)

Juvenile

Slingjaw Wrasse *Epibulus insidiator.* Size: to 35cm

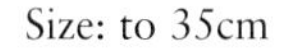

Young male

Mature male

Dark colour variant

Female

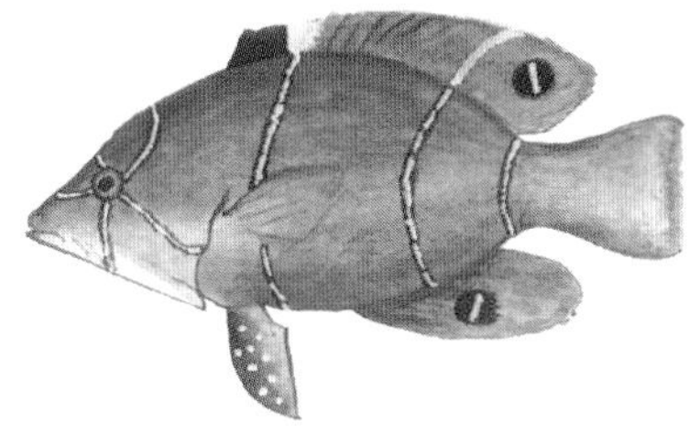

Juvenile

Solitary, sometimes sexes paired. Wary of divers, particularly when young. Juveniles seldom seen in the open. Painting of juvenile by author from specimen in authors' aquarium.

Pallas, 1770

Cigar Wrasse *Cheilio inermis*

Size: to 50cm

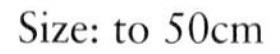

Female

Male

Not very common, difficult to approach. Found singly, in pairs or groups, on top of the reef, at the base and in the shallow seagrass areas. Colour may vary from brown to green or yellow. Pink area near pectoral fin found only on mature males. The yellow form has often been observed 'riding' larger fishes.

Forsskål, 1775

Red Sea Bird Wrasse *Gomphosus caeruleus klunzingeri*

Size: to 25cm

Female

Male

Juvenile

The Red Sea variant of *G. caeruleus* found in the Indian Ocean. Fast moving, ever active fish.

Klausewitz, 1962

Nebulous Wrasse *Halichoeres nebulosus*

Size: to 11cm

Rarely seen, probably because it blends well with the coral background.

Valenciennes, 1839

Male with female

Female

Checkerboard Wrasse *Halichoeres hortulanus*

Size: to 25cm

Male

Female

Common, and often curious of divers. Very opportunistic and will follow bottom feeders, such as Goatfish.

Lacepede, 1801

Juvenile

Dusky Wrasse *Halichoeres marginatus.*

Size: to 17cm

Male

Female

Common in shallower areas of coral. Very elusive.

Ruppell, 1835

Juvenile

Zigzag Wrasse *Halichoeres scapularis*

Size: to 20cm

Mature male

Very common, particularly over sandy areas. Mature males have a different colour pattern in the Red Sea to that in the Indo Pacific region.

Bennett, 1831

Barred Wrasse *Hemigymnus fasciatus*

Size: to 45cm

Solitary. Width and pattern of bars vary. Large breeding males may exhibit a reversal of the black and white bands.

Bloch, 1792

Juvenile

Thicklip Wrasse *Hemigymnus melapterus*

Size: to 50cm

Solitary, though sometimes seen paired. Mature individuals assume overall grey/green colour.

Bloch, 1791

Juvenile

Ring Wrasse *Hologymnosus annulatus*

Size: to 40cm

Adult

Sub-adult

Adults solitary, juveniles often swim in groups. Very active fish.

Lacepède, 1802

Juvenile

Fourline Wrasse *Larabicus quadrilineatus*

Size: to 11cm

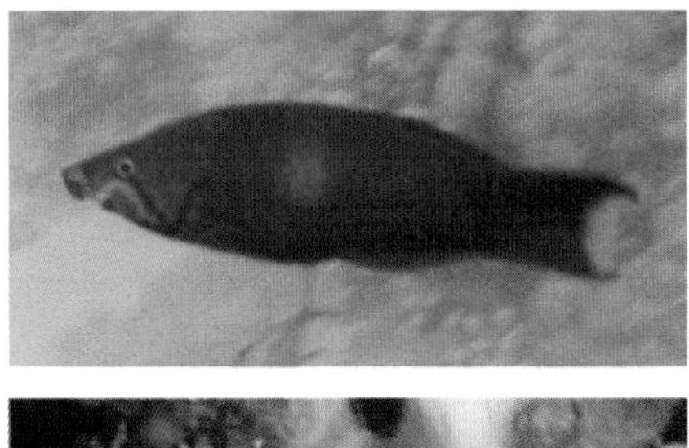

Red Sea and Arabian peninsula only. Juveniles resemble the Cleaner Wrasse juvenile and are active cleaners. The adult male has no lateral stripes, but develops a curved line under the eye. It has also been seen with a yellow stripe in its dorsal fin.

Ruppell, 1835

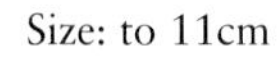

Cleaner Wrasse *Labroides dimidiatus*

Size: to 11cm

Very common, maintains a cleaning station.

Valenciennes, 1839

Juvenile

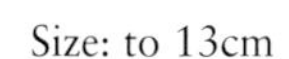

Vermiculate Wrasse *Macropharyngodon biparitus marisrubri*

Size: to 13cm

Female

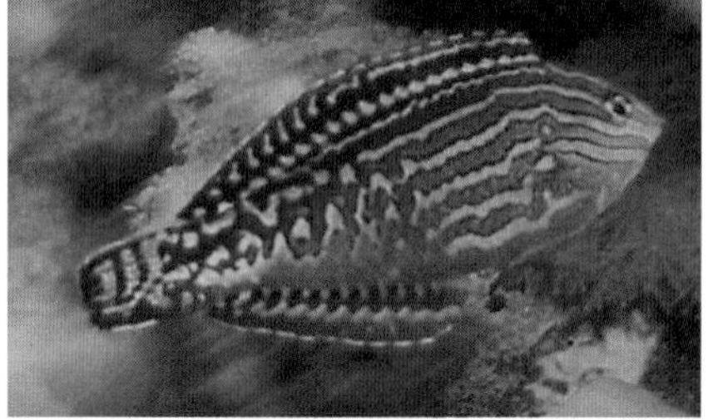

Male

A distinct Red Sea variant of the IndoPacific species. Solitary, though females may be in groups.

Randall, 1978

Rockmover Wrasse *Novaculichthys taeniourus*

Size: to 27cm

Solitary, and approachable when feeding. It turns over rocks of considerable size stirring up clouds of sand, which attracts many freeloaders.

Lacepède, 1801

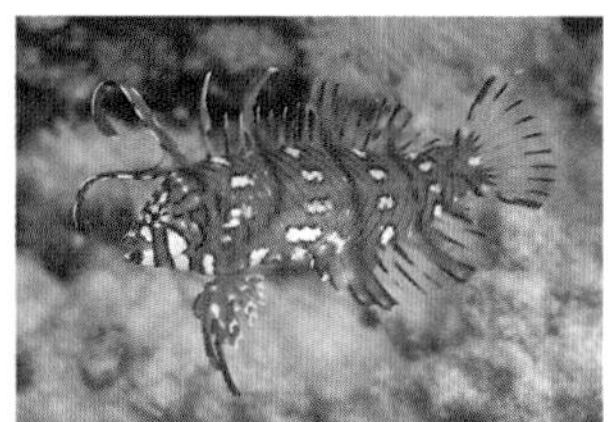

Juvenile

Bandcheek Wrasse *Oxycheilinus Digrammus*

Size: to 30cm

Striped colour form

Mature male

Adult

Common, particularly on the first shelf. Unafraid of divers, and inquisitive.

Lacepède, 1802

Mental Wrasse *Oxycheilinus mentalis*

Size: to 18cm

Mature male

Striped form

Mimic group

Solitary and common; juveniles may be observed hiding in soft coral. This Wrasse can cleverly adapt it's colour pattern to imitate Goatfishes. It will then feed with them on the bottom. This colour pattern change is shown. The Mental Wrasse is frequently mistaken as the Bandcheek. The Mental always has a white area on the caudal peduncle, which the Bandcheek lacks.

Bennett, 1828

Eightline Wrasse *Paracheilinus octotaenia*

Size: to 9cm

Male breeding colours

Female

Male

Red Sea only. Common at first shelf and below. Breeding males exhibit very vivid colours and 'flash' their fins in display to the groups of females. Fishes of this genus are sometimes referred to as 'Flashers'.

Fourmanoir, 1955

Disappearing Wrasse *Pseudocheilinus evanidus*

Size: to 8cm

Solitary and associated with soft coral. Very cautious.

Jordan & Evermann, 1903

Sixstripe Wrasse *Pseudocheilinus hexataenia*

Size: to 6cm

Numerous within coral branches, but very elusive. Sometimes found in anemones.

Bleeker, 1857

Chiseltooth Wrasse *Pseudodax moluccanus*

Size: to 25cm

Solitary, fairly common. Easily identified by its white teeth and yellow upper lip.

Cuvier & Valenciennes, 1840

Juvenile

Cryptic Wrasse *Pteragogus cryptus*

Size: to 7cm

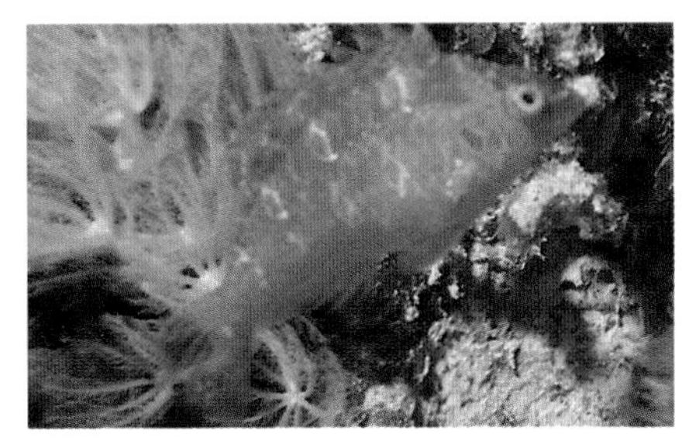

Not often seen; a very wary fish which will hide in soft coral at any suggestion of danger. The additional photo is presumed to be of the same species, although it shows unusually strong markings.

Randall, 1981

Bluelined Wrasse *Stethojulis albovittata*

Size: to 12cm

Female

Male

Often seen in the shallows; very fast moving and difficult to approach.

Bonnaterre, 1788

Cutribbon Wrasse *Stethojulis interrupta*

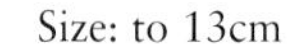
Size: to 13cm

Juvenile shown.
Adults resemble the Bluelined Wrasse.

Bleeker, 1851

Klunzinger's Wrasse *Thalassoma klunzingeri*

Size: to 20cm

Red Sea only. Particularly active on the top of reefs. Juveniles have a very prominent red basal bar.

Fowler & Steinitz, 1956

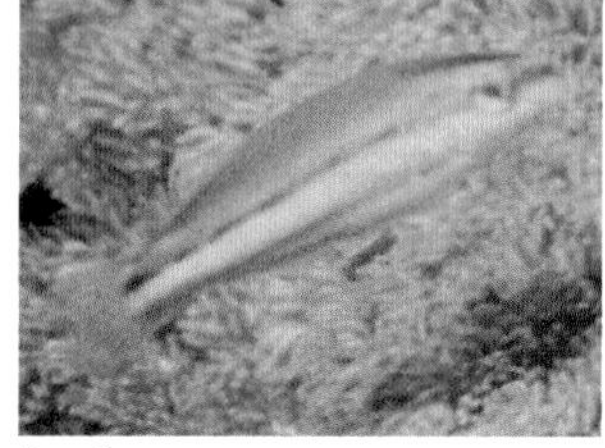

Juvenile

Moon Wrasse *Thalassoma lunare*

Size: to 25cm

Solitary or groups of juveniles. Females are bright green with yellow in the tail, males are bluish with white tail inset.

Linnaeus, 1758

Juvenile

Surge Wrasse *Thalassoma purpureum*

Size: to 40cm

Not very common.
Very active; found over shallow coral reef exposed to wave action. Mature males may be mistaken for Parrotfish owing to their blue/pink colour.

Forsskål, 1775

Female

Pygmy Wrasse *Wetmorella nigropinnata*

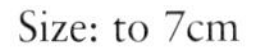

Size: to 7cm

Juvenile

Rarely seen; hides in the dark shadows of the seaward reef faces, seldom venturing away from safety. The juvenile bears a close resemblance to the juvenile Slingjaw Wrasse, but has an additional vertical bar.

Seale, 1901

Razorfish *Xyrichtys pavo*

Size: to 40cm

Juvenile shown. Solitary and shy. Found in flat sandy areas. The adults of *X. pavo* are pale beige/green with a blunt head and eyes high up. Adults are found usually below 30m.

Valenciennes 1840

African Coris *Coris africana*

Size: to 38cm

Early Juvenile

Late Juvenile

Solitary, not common. Mature males have pale bar above origin of anal fin. Previously referred to as *C. gaimardi*; this name is now reserved for the eastern Indian Ocean form.

Quoy & Gaimard, 1824

Clown Coris *Coris aygula*

Size: to 60cm

Juvenile

Female

Male

The largest Coris, usually solitary but sometimes paired. Cautious of divers. Believed to sleep buried in sand.

Lacepède, 1802

Spottail Coris *Coris caudimacula*

Size: to 20cm

Female

Male

Not common on the reef, but will be seen at the base usually over sand. Both sexes can adopt pattern of broad vertical bars, which is also the juvenile's marking.

Quoy & Gaimard, 1834

Dapple Coris *Coris variegata*

Size: to 20cm

Usually solitary.
It will often follow divers.

Ruppell, 1835

Juvenile

Lyretail Hogfish *Bodianus anthioides*

Size: to 24cm

Usually solitary, juveniles sometimes grouped. The most common Hogfish. It will often be seen 'blowing' sand to reveal food.

Bennett, 1831

Juvenile

Axilspot Hogfish *Bodianus axillaris*

Size: to 21cm

Juvenile

Female

Male

Invariably solitary.
Adult males seen more often than females.

Bennett, 1831

Diana's Hogfish *Bodianus diana*

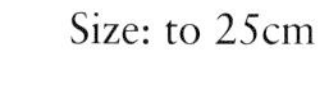

Size: to 25cm

Solitary and cautious.

Lacepède, 1802

Panther Flounder *Bothus pantherinus*

Size: to 30cm

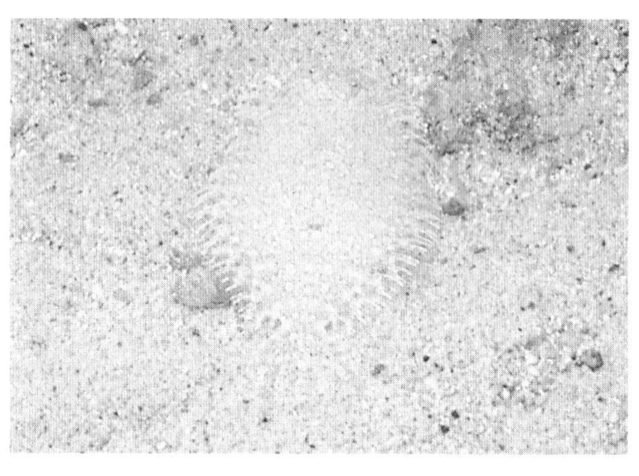

Common, but usually overlooked since well camouflaged against the sandy bottom - will be seen at all depths within amateur diving range.

Rüppell, 1830

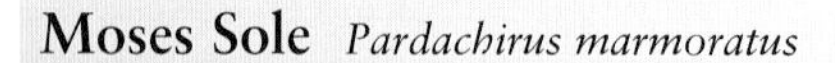

Moses Sole *Pardachirus marmoratus*

Size: to 26cm

Found on sandy bottoms in shallows, often partially buried.

Lacepède, 1802

There are reported to be 12 species of Flounder in the Red Sea, and 10 of Sole. The Moses Sole *(Pardachirus marmoratus)* is probably the only species of Sole that will be seen by recreational divers and snorkellers. The fisherman should note that it has toxic glands and a very bitter skin.

Both Flounders and Soles are carnivorous.

Flounders (Bothidae)		**Soles** (Soleidae)	
Arnoglossus	*marisrubri*	*Aesopia*	*heterorhina*
Bothus	*pantherinus*	*Pardachirus*	*marmoratus*
		Soleichthys	*heterorhinos*

(Psettodidae)
Psettodes *erumei*[1]

1 Not found near reefs

Puffer & Porcupinefishes

Pufferfishes are common in all reef areas in the Red Sea, with the Masked Pufferfish being perhaps the most prevalent. They are known also as Blowfishes, and the smaller species as Tobies. There are 15 species of Pufferfish reported in the Red Sea, 3 of which are the much smaller Tobies.

The Indian Ocean contains approximately 30 species of Pufferfish and 10 of Porcupinefish. Of the 30 Pufferfishes, 13 are sharp-nose Pufferfishes (i.e. Tobies).

Species are characterised by their soft-rayed fins and lack of pelvic fins. They have prominent rear dorsal and anal fins. The Pufferfishes have smooth, tough skins, whilst Porcupinefishes have in addition numerous small spikes all over its body.

The origin of the name Pufferfish is popularly attributed to its ability to rapidly draw water (or air when raised out of the water) into its abdomen to expand its scaleless body into almost spherical proportions. This is a defensive action to deter predators, amply demonstrated to us on an occasion when we observed a very large Grouper apparently attacking a Masked Pufferfish - the Pufferfish inflated almost instantaneously, whereupon the Grouper quickly fled.

The alternative name of Blowfish we believe to be more appropriate, as it describes an activity which I have observed in larger species. This activity is one of 'blowing' soft sediment or sand to reveal hidden molluscs and invertebrates (this is a technique adopted by treasure seekers in their exploration of wreck surrounds using large reverse vacuum cleaners!).

Pufferfishes are equipped with very strong, beak-like fused teeth which enable

Blue edged Sole *Soleichthys heterorhinos*

Size: to 15cm

Found in shallow water.
Active at night.

Bleeker, 1856

Masked Pufferfish *Arothron diadematus*

Size: to 30cm

Very common; shows considerable colour variation, sometimes very dark blue/grey.

Rüppell, 1829

Bristly Pufferfish *Arothron hispidus*

Size: to 35cm

Quite common;
Red Sea population differs from the rest of the IndoPacific in having more spots.

Linnaeus, 1758

them to break mollusc shells. A diver finding a Pufferfish in its reef lair will find a carpet of broken shells inside. The diet of Pufferfishes is very varied, which makes them undesirable aquarium animals. They will eat not only molluscs but starfish, sea urchins, sponges and any worthwhile invertebrate. They are also dangerous in the aquarium in that they carry a toxin in their organs which can poison themselves or other fish (the Japanese consider the flesh as a delicacy, though clearly, it is more a challenge than a delight to eat!).

Unfortunately, Pufferfishes (and more often Porcupinefishes) are well known in some parts of the tourist world, particularly S.E.Asia, as rather grotesque lampshades.

There has been a noticeable decline in the number of Porcupinefishes that can be seen on the fringing reefs (their favourite habitat) which may be linked to the decline in molluscs in the adjacent lagoons.

In their own environment, Pufferfishes and Porcupinefishes are a delight to observe. They are ungainly and slow in movement, and will study a diver warily through large, dark, cowlike eyes. A curious Porcupinefish will often follow a swimmer, seemingly playing a hide-and-seek game along the fringing reef.

The Masked Pufferfish can be quite comical in appearance - following distension of its abdomen, it has rolls of loose flesh around its belly - the large black eyepatches contribute to the overall appearance of an overweight carnival character.

Pufferfishes (Tetraodontidae)
Arothron *diadematus*[1]
Arothron *hispidus*
Arothron *stellatus*
Arothron *sordidus*
Amblyrhinchotes *hypselogeneion*
Torquigener *flavimaculosus*

Tobys (Canthigasteridae)
Canthigaster *coronata*
Canthigaster *margaritata*[1]
Canthigaster *pygmaea*[1]

Porcupinefishes (Diodontidae)
Diodon *holocanthus*
Diodon *hystrix*
Diodon *liturosus*
Chilomycterus *spilostylus*

1 Red Sea species

Triggerfishes & Filefishes

Triggerfishes and Filefishes are closely related, and share some common characteristics.

Of particular note, species of both families are characterised by their distinctive trigger (or file) like dorsal, which in the case of Triggerfishes is actually composed

Stellate Pufferfish *Arothron stellatus*

Size: to 120cm

Adopts camouflage colouration when resting on the sea floor. Juveniles yellow/orange with spots similar to adults.

Bloch & Schneider, 1801

Crown Toby *Canthigaster coronata*

Size: to 13cm

Not very common; mostly seen below 15m.

Vaillant & Sauvage, 1875

Pearl Toby *Canthigaster margaritata*

Size: to 12cm

There appear to be several colour and pattern variations in this species.

Rüppell, 1829

Pygmy Toby *Canthigaster pygmaea*

Size: to 6cm

Rare: secretive.

Allen & Randall, 1977

Common Porcupinefish *Diodon hystrix*

Size: to 70cm

Very common, especially at the edge of reefs. May also be found in very shallow water.

Linnaeus, 1758

Blackblotched Porcupinefish *Diodon liturosus*

Size: to 50cm

Rare; hides amongst coral, sometimes deep. Photographed at El Erg, n. Red Sea.

Shaw, 1804.

of three webbed spines, the rearmost acting as a lock for the long mid spine. The Triggerfish carries these dorsal spines behind the level of its eyes.

Filefishes have a single long dorsal spine, with a very small one at its base. This dorsal is either directly above the eye, or slightly forward of it.

Triggerfishes have a smooth, sometimes shiny, appearance since they are covered by small scales, whereas Filefishes have a 'furry' look as a result of each of their small scales having an extended small spine. Certain species of each group have rows of small scutes at the base of their tails.

Judging by their behaviour in the aquarium, and despite their appearance (high eyes, negligible forehead) one could believe that Triggerfishes possess a level of intelligence higher than many of their marine cohabitants. This may be an impression gained from the attitude of the Triggerfish, which ranges from complete indifference to violent aggressiveness. As aquarium fish they can become pets, responding vigorously to mealtimes and enjoying being stroked. They are also very useful, since they will raise food from the bottom, ingest it, break it up and then eject it as a cloud of small pieces, which smaller fish eagerly snatch. No aquarium should be without one of these comic characters.

Triggerfishes are found all along the fringing reef - some are found only in relatively deep water (such as the Blue, or Yellowmargin Triggerfish), whilst the Picasso is most plentiful in the shallow lagoon areas. The Picasso is a Red Sea species, and will always be seen in the shallow areas - when it runs for cover, it will hide in a sandy crevice and 'lock' itself in by extending its strong dorsal. It is a comic character - when it feels that it is safe to emerge, it will slowly leave its sanctuary, tail first! It is coloured to match the sandy areas that it appears to prefer, but the three black horizontal lines marking rows of small scutes at the base of its tail will always give its hiding place away.

The Blue and the Titan Triggerfishes can grow to a considerable size. They are 'heavy' fishes and when they reach 0.5m they can be intimidating. These are both fishes that the diver learns to avoid. The Titan will bite, without being provoked, and in our experience without necessarily being in the vicinity of its nest site. Our son can testify to this aggressive behaviour, having spent many minutes battling with a particularly persistent individual.

Juvenile Triggerfishes are attractively coloured, with the Blue Triggerfish being the most striking. Despite being a deeper water species, Blue Triggerfish juveniles will be seen in the inshore lagoon areas.

As a general statement, Triggerfishes are solitary fish. There are, however, exceptions, one of which is the Red Tooth which forms large aggregations off the fringing reef, feeding on plankton. These fish can crowd a diver in areas where they have been hand fed. They are so called for their reddish upper teeth, and lower teeth red with a yellow base. At night they sleep in crevices on the side of the reef, close together and forming small pockets of blue green colour.

The diet of Triggerfishes is varied - with their strong jaws they are able to crush mollusc shells and crabs and they will energetically tackle sea urchins and star fish. The Titan is known to be a predator of the Crown of Thorns starfish, which is

Yellow spotted Burrfish *Chilomycterus spilostylus*

Size: to 35cm

Solitary, not often seen in the open water.

Leis and Randall, 1982

Orangestriped Triggerfish *Balistapus undulatus*

Size: to 30cm

A common species found on reef face and first shelf. Often the lines will be broken up into dots. Adult males have no markings on snout.

Mungo-Park, 1797

Titan Triggerfish *Balistoides viridescens*

Size: to 75cm

The largest species. It can be aggressive towards divers, particularly when guarding eggs. They will often circle divers in open water.

Bloch & Schneider, 1801

Redtooth Triggerfish *Odonus niger*

Size: to 30cm

Common along reef faces. They form large schools.

Rüppell, 1836

Yellowmargin Triggerfish *Pseudobalistes flavimarginatus*

Size: to 60cm

Similar to Titan, but less aggressive.

Rüppell, 1829

Blue Triggerfish *Pseudobalistes fuscus*

Size: to 55cm

The most cautious of the larger species. Usually found below 20m. Juveniles are yellow with blue markings.

Bloch & Schneider, 1801

Picasso Triggerfish *Rhinecanthus assasi*

Size: to 30cm

Very common in lagoon areas. Large specimens may be found occasionally below 20m.

Forsskål, 1775

Bluethroat Triggerfish *Sufflamen albicaudatus*

Size: to 20cm

Red Sea variant of *S. crysopterus*. A small species, common along the first shelf. Older individuals with vertical yellow stripe behind eye, rarely seen.

Rüppell, 1829

Bridled Triggerfish *Sufflamen fraenatus*

Size: to 38cm

Rare in the Red Sea.
Adult develops pale yellow ring around mouth and yellow band across chin. Authors' aquarium photograph.

Latreille, 1804

Scrawled Filefish *Aluterus scriptus*

Size: to 80cm

Largest Filefish, rarely seen, difficult to approach, mostly solitary sometimes in small groups

Osbeck, 1765

Broom Filefish *Amanses scopas*

Size: to 20cm

Males have 5-6 long dark spines, females have a mass of brush (or broom)-like projections at the back of the body.

Cuvier, 1829

Wire-net Filefish *Cantherhines pardalis*

Size: to 20cm

Juvenile

Several colour forms but they all have the white spot behind the dorsal fin

Rüppell, 1837

Harlequin Filefish *Oxymonacanthus halli*

Size: to 7cm

In pairs or groups; graze on coral polyps; Red Sea variant of *O. longinostris*. Males have an orange spot on pelvic fins.

Marshall, 1952

Mimic Filefish *Paraluteres arqat*

Size: to 10cm

Toby

Mimic

Rare. The mimic is a very close copy of Toby *Canthigaster margaritata* (shown in adjacent photo). Other fish know that *C. margaritata* is toxic. Seldom raises its trigger so avoiding breaking the disguise. The distinguishing features are the length of dorsal and anal fins.

Clark & Gohar, 1953

Cube Trunkfish *Ostracion cubicus*

Size: to 45cm

Common and solitary.

Linnaeus, 1758

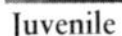

Juvenile

Mature male

difficult to imagine as easy prey. Smaller Triggerfishes will sometimes be seen grazing on coral polyps.

Although Triggerfishes do not as a general rule change their colours significantly according to environment or circumstances (other than becoming paler at night) the Bluethroat Triggerfish does appear at times to change the colour of its caudal fin from the usual yellow inset to deep brown/black.

Triggerfishes have a characteristic style of swimming - the larger species of Titan and Yellowmargin will swim inclined to 45 degrees when they see a diver, with one eye fixed on the intruder. They all swim using their large second dorsal and anal fins, which provide movement by a rippling action.

Filefishes are not as approachable as Triggerfishes; they are very cautious and will invariably swim away from divers. Although there are 13 species reported in the Red Sea, only the Broom, Wirenet and the Harlequin Filesfishes will be seen regularly.

The Broom and the Wirenet will be observed mainly on the fringing reef and down to the first shelf. The Harlequin, a small attractively coloured fish, will be seen, usually in small groups, on the fringing reef, moving from coral head to coral head feeding on its preferred food of coral polyps.

The Scrawled Filefish is the largest of the Filefishes - it is not often seen, since it is both rare and secretive. It is immediately recognised by its very heavy robust tail (looking somewhat like the tail of a Pufferfish), pointed snout and blue scrawl-like markings. The authors have watched one of these fish repeatedly nudging a small jellyfish, apparently in an attempt to eat it.

Filefishes will sometimes be found in seagrass beds, in particular the Wirenet.

Species in the genus *Paraluteres* are remarkable mimics of Tobies - Tobies are respected by predators since they are known to be toxic, and species of *Paraluteres* Filefish adopt a Toby's colour form as a disguise. They will also keep their Trigger embedded to complete the imitation. *P. arqat* copies *Canthigaster margaritata* (shown in the photograph section); it is extremely difficult to discern the mimic from the Toby. The most obvious visual difference is that the mimic has a greater number of fin rays, most noticeably in the dorsal fin.

Triggerfish (Balistidae)		**Filefish** (Monacanthidae)	
Balistapus	*undulatus*	*Aluterus*	*scriptus*
Balistoides	*viridescens*	*Amanses*	*scopas*
Melichthys	*indicus*[2]	*Brachaluteres*	*fahaqa*
Odonus	*niger*	*Cantherhines*	*pardalis*
Pseudobalistes	*flavimarginatus*	*Oxymonacanthus*	*halli*[1]
Pseudobalistes	*fuscus*	*Paramonacanthus*	*barnadi*
Rhinecanthus	*assasi*[1]	*Paraluteres*	*arqat*[1]
Sufflamen	*albicaudatus*	*Stephanolepsis*	*diasporos*
Sufflamen	*fraenatus*	*Thamnaconus*	*modestoides erythraeensis*

1 Red Sea species
2 Reported in the Southern Red Sea (Indian Triggerfish)

Bluetail Trunkfish *Ostracion cyanurus*

Size: to 15cm

Common all over the reef; solitary.

Rüppell, 1828

Juvenile

Thornback Trunkfish *Tetrosomus gibbosus*

Size: to 30cm

Not common, solitary. Pictured blowing sand to reveal small invertebrates.

Linnaeus, 1758

Orangespotted Jack *Carangoides bajad*

Size: to 53cm

Very common near reefs, singly or in small groups. Can change colour to all yellow. Inquisitive fish, which will often approach divers.

Forsskål, 1775

Trunkfishes

Trunkfishes (also known as Boxfishes) are allied to the Puffer and Porcupinefishes, and share a number of characteristics of their cousins. They are slow moving, ungainly creatures whose prime engines of movement are the strong, although spineless, dorsal and anal fins.

They differ from the Pufferfishes in having a hard exterior box-like covering composed of bony plates, with gaps for tail, gills, mouth and anus. This turtle-like carapace varies in cross section from species to species, and can be triangular, rectangular or even pentangular.

Although there are known to be at least 15 species of Trunkfish in the Indian Ocean, only 4 have been reported in the Red Sea. The most frequently seen is the Bluetail, which can be quite plentiful in localised areas. Unlike its larger relatives, the Bluetail prefers to live amongst the coral - others are bottom dwelling.

Trunkfish have small mouths, often protruding, surrounded by thick fleshy lips. They are omnivorous and will graze on soft as well as hard corals. The odd Thornback Trunkfish, with its triangular armour, has been observed 'blowing' sand in the same manner as a Pufferfish, to reveal small creatures in the sand.

Whilst their first line of defence is their armour plating, they also carry a skin toxin - they are clearly an unattractive proposition for predators.

Trunkfishes (Ostraciidae)

Ostracion	*cubicus*	*Tetrosomus*	*gibbosus*
Ostracion	*cyanurus* [1]	*Lactoria*	*cornuta* [2]

1 Red Sea species 2 Southern Red Sea

Open Water Fishes

Although a greater part of the piscatorial life in the Red Sea revolves directly around the coral reefs, there is a large variety of open water pelagic fishes which divers and snorkellers will encouter. These can range in size from the huge Whale Shark to the little flying fish that panic as the dive boat approaches them. Many, however, of the pelagic fishes are highly specialised, sleek silvery creatures with a fast turn of speed - these fishes are typically the Tunas, Jacks and Barracudas, all of which are voracious predators of smaller fishes, and which occasionally visit reefs to forage, usually in small schools of perhaps a dozen fish; a school of Barracuda, however, may contain hundreds. These fish are designed for speed and endurance and can travel long distances in a short time. To be out at sea and to observe a great commotion on the water surface, with wheeling seabirds squabbling above, demonstrates how fast and furious are their feeding habits. These fishes are the wolves of the sea, fearless of man and magnificent to observe.

Sevenbar Jack *Carangoides ferdau*

Size: to 70cm

Common off the reef face, invariably in small schools.

Forsskål, 1775

Yellowspotted Jack *Carangoides fulvoguttatus*

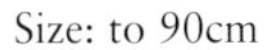

Size: to 90cm

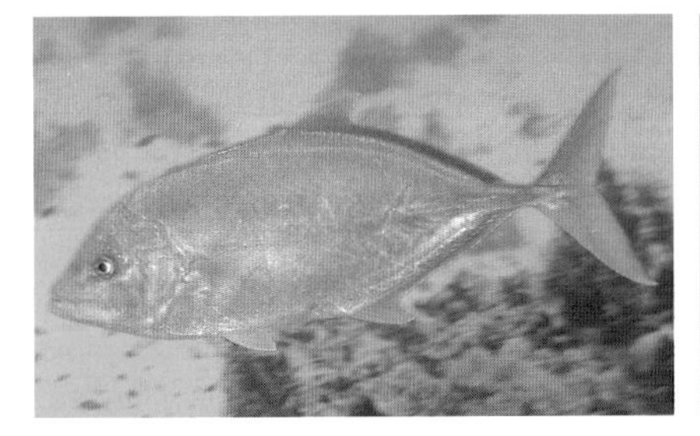

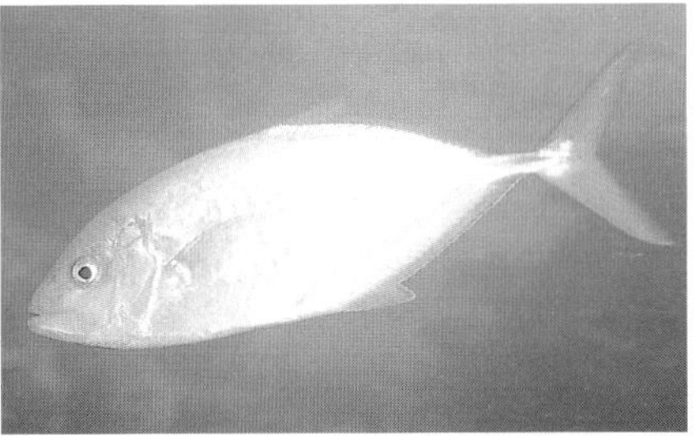

Common, usually in small groups. Larger individuals have less prominent spots.

Forsskål,1775

Bluefin Trevally *Caranx melampygus*

Size: to 100cm

Usually seen in small marauding groups, although they can form huge schools. Very inquisitive of divers, and quite fearless.

Cuvier, 1833

We were once fortunate to see a Trevally of such a size off Port Sudan to have an attendant scavenging shark of 2m in length! During night fishing in the same location, our heavy wooden hulled felucca was towed 2 miles by an enormous Tuna!

Many of the pelagic fish are inquisitive creatures that will come to investigate divers - in unclear water the sudden appearance of a school of fast swimming large silvery Jacks can be quite stimulating. Often they will circle the diver in open water, in obvious puzzlement at this strange sea creature!

Jacks are significant food fishes in the region, and provide good sport for line and spear fishermen alike. They are excellent to eat, particularly when cooked fresh over an open fire.

The name 'Jack' covers a very broad range of species, mainly in the *Carangoides, Scomberoides* and *Caranx* genus. There are at least 22 species in the Red Sea that are loosely called Jacks - the most commonly seen is the Orange Spotted *(Carangoides bajad)*. The name bajad is derived from the arabic name used generally to describe fishes of this type, in much the same way that the name Jack is used in English.

It is not always an easy task to establish the identity of these species - they look very similar in shape and usually have a uniform silver appearance. Colour changes do, however, occur - the Orange Spotted Jack can be all silver, spotted or all bright yellow, and some species have very different juvenile forms. The small, black-barred pilot fishes often seen with sharks and other large fishes is the young Golden Toothless Trevally.

Whilst Jacks may show interest in divers, Barracudas are unnervingly the most inquisitive, and will frequently follow a diver, even up to the shore line. They are invariably present, but often unnoticed, along the fringing and outer reefs.

There are 5 species of Barracuda known in the Red Sea, and most are shoaling species. The most impressive, however, is the solitary Great Barracuda which is frequently seen, and which can be as long as 2m. Like many large predators, it is fearless and can be approached with ease (and with a strong heart!). Very often, when diving off the shore early in the day, large schools of small Barracuda may be seen in the shallows - presumably resting after a hard night's work. At night these Barracuda can be a menace to fishermen - when fishing near a school they will bite seconds after the bait enters the water, making it impossible to fish at depth.

Many of the reef sharks sleep during the day in reef caverns - once whilst snorkelling on the fringing reef I dived to investigate what I thought was a strange kelp-like growth projecting from the reef edge; it materialised as the tail of a large reef shark asleep in a reef-edge cave.

There are some 30 species of shark known to inhabit the Red Sea - around the Jeddah area however, they are very seldom seen - it is indeed an event to come across one. There is one individual, a Silky Shark of about 2.5m in length, which appears to be locally resident, and which has been seen by many divers at popular offshore reefs. It is a species described as semi pelagic, so it appears strange that it should be seen in the same area repeatedly. On one occasion when I came across

Bigeye Trevally *Caranx sexfasciatus*

Size: to 85cm

Common, usually in large schools. Juveniles carry dark bands (six), hence the specific name. Identified by the black spot at the top of the opercle.

Quoy & Gaimard, 1825

Golden Toothless Trevally *Gnathanodon speciosus*

Size: to 120cm

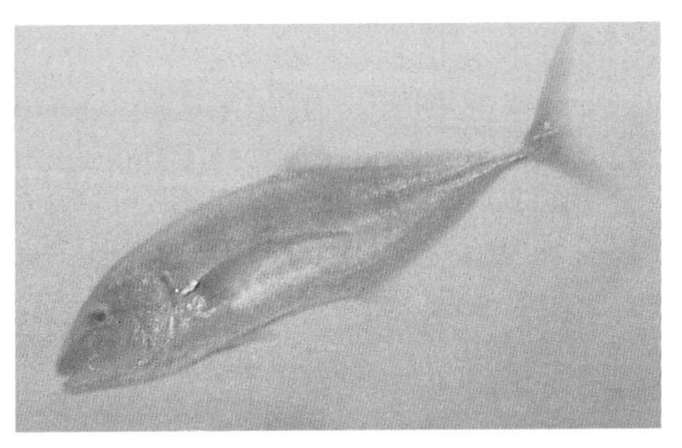

Juveniles heavily plumed. Develop vertical black bands and lose them with age. Older individuals lose their teeth. Primary juveniles associated with jellyfish, secondary juveniles with sharks.

Forsskål, 1775

Great Barracuda *Sphyraena barracuda*

Size: to 200cm

Usually solitary; maintains a station off the reef edge over deep water, and will hunt on top of the reef. Solitary individuals will approach divers - it is said that they are attracted to bright objects which divers may carry.

Walbaum, 1792

this particular shark I ventured very close to obtain photographs, only to discover later that I had no film in the camera!

Dolphins are a familiar sight in the Red Sea. Although we all love these creatures, and many of us wish to be in the water with them, I suggest that divers and snorkellers alike should not assume that pelagic Sharks will not be near a pod of Dolphin.

Just off the fringing reef the water is rich in planktonic material - it is there that the ghostly shoals of silver Striped Mackerel feed. These Mackerel *(Rastelliger kanagurta)* form very large shoals, with individuals tightly packed together. They swim as one, very slowly and with their mouths agape, filtering the water for plankton.

The Striped Mackerel's much larger relative, the solitary Spanish Mackerel *(Scomberomorus commerson)* will also be found off the reef. I have observed one specimen of about 1.5m with a retinue of some 20 small Jacks trailing behind, picking up the leftovers.

When boat diving, it is always worthwhile to investigate passing jellyfish, which will sometimes have small fish hiding in their trailing tentacles. The juvenile Golden Trevally *(Gnathanodon speciosus)* often travels in this way, covering great distances with its protector. This particular Trevally, in its next stage of development (vertically banded) will change host and swim with large pelagic species, such as sharks.

Jacks (Carangidae)

Alectis	*indicus*
Alepes	*djedaba*
Atule	*mate*
Carangoides	*armatus*
Carangoides	*bajad*
Carangoides	*chrysoptera*
Carangoides	*caeruleopinnatus*
Carangoides	*compressus*
Carangoides	*diversa*
Carangoides	*ferdau*
Carangoides	*fulvoguttatus*
Carangoides	*gymnostethus*
Carangoides	*malabaricus*
Carangoides	*plagiotaenia*
Elagatis	*bipinnulatus*
Scomberoides	*tol*
Scomberoides	*commersonianus*
Scomberoides	*lysan*
Trachinotus	*blochii*
Ulua	*mentalis*

Barracuda (Sphyraenidae)

Sphyraena	*barracuda*
Sphyraena	*flavicauda*
Sphyraena	*forsteri*
Sphyraena	*jello*
Sphyraena	*obtusata*
Sphyraena	*putnamiae*
Sphyraena	*qenie*

Tuna & Mackerel (Scombridae)

Euthynnus	*affinis*
Gymnosarda	*unicolor*
Thunnus	*albacares*
Thunnus	*tonggol*
Katsuwonus	*pelamis*
Scomberomorus	*commerson*
Rastelliger	*kanagurta*
Auxis	*thazard*

Blackfin Barracuda *Sphyraena qenie*

Size: to 160cm

A schooling species, but is sometimes seen singly.
Prefers areas of strong currents.

Klunzinger, 1870

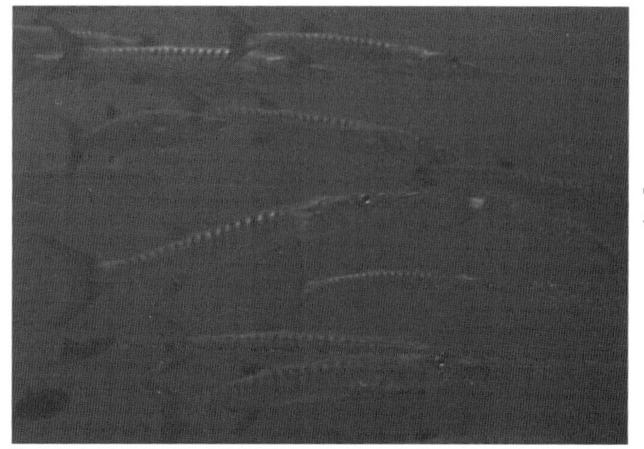

Dogtooth Tuna *Gymnosarda unicolor*

Size: to 220cm

Often seen in pairs swimming along the side of reefs.

Rüppell, 1836

Yellowfin Tuna *Thunnus albacares*

Size: to 200cm

Usually seen in schools, though sometimes singly.

Bonnaterre, 1788

Caranx	*ignoblis*
Caranx	*melampygus*
Caranx	*sexfasciatus*
Gnathanodon	*speciosus*

Cobia (Rachycentridae)

Rachycentron	*canadum*

Bonefish (Albulidae)

Albula	*vulpes*

Flying Fish (Exoetidae)

Exocoetus	*volitans*

Halfbeaks (Hemiramphidae)

Hemiramphus	*far*
Hemiramphus	*marginatus*
Hyporhamphus	*acutus*
Hyporhamphus	*gamberur*[1]

Houndfish, Needlefish (Belonidae)

Platybelone	*argalus*
Tylosurus	*choram*
Tylosurus	*crocodilus*

1 Red Sea species

Inshore Fishes

The rich variety of fish life that exists in the sandy lagoon areas that divide the shore and the fringing reef is often overlooked in our haste to view the vivid colours and activity of the fringing reef - when walking out to the reef from the shore, an occasional look in the shallow water can bring some pleasant surprises. Many species of fishes live permanently in these shallow areas, and will not be seen beyond the fringing reef. These areas are also a nursery for many juvenile reef fishes, and they offer an opportunity to study the youngsters at close range.

There can be some surprises too - amazingly large Porcupinefish may be found hiding in holes or under small coral outcrops. A Snake Eel may be discovered, head buried in sand searching for small crustaceans, or some large Jacks may flash past at speed in water barely deeper than their body depth.

The lagoon areas along the mid Saudi Arabia coastline are mostly sand bottomed with coral outcrops and small areas of seagrass. The depth of water along the coastline can be very shallow, so that under certain conditions of wind and tide, vast areas of the lagoon area are exposed to the searing heat and sunshine. Incredibly, animal life in general appears to survive this natural hardship, although there are of course casualties, particularly amongst the mollusc communities - after a few days exposure to the sun, the lagoon area can be a shell collectors paradise.

Striped Mackerel *Rastelliger kanagurta*

Size: to 35cm

Form large schools and feed on planktonic matter along reef edges, with their mouths wide open.

Cuvier, 1816

Spanish Mackerel *Scomberomorus commerson*

Size: to 220cm

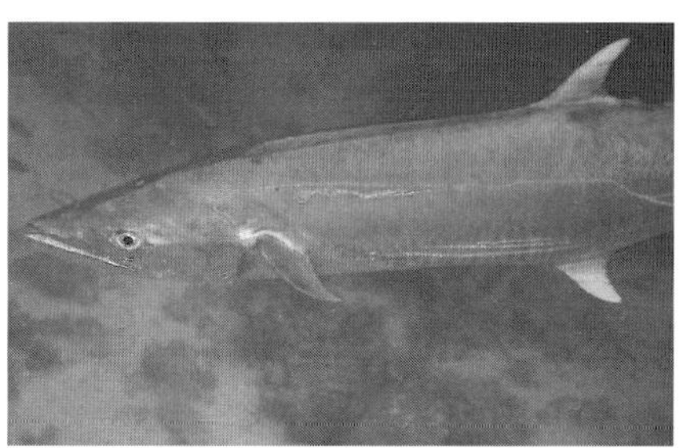

Solitary species, largest of the Mackerels.

Lacepède, 1800

Red Sea Houndfish *Tylosurus choram*

Size: to 120cm

A solitary species found in the Red Sea and Mediterranean only. Swims just below the surface near reefs.

Rüppell, 1837

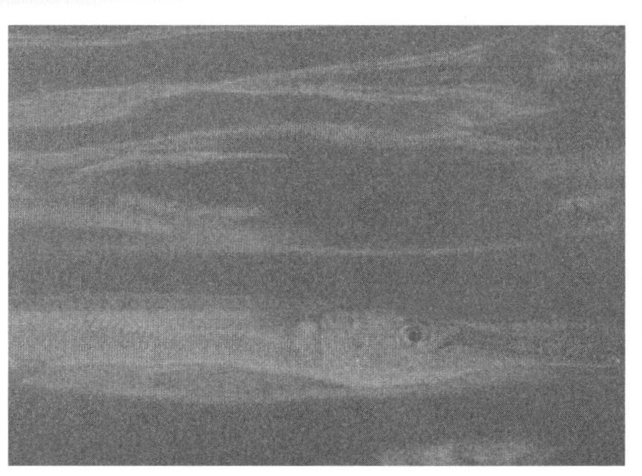

The seagrass areas of the lagoons are home to many adult fishes, which are often very secretive and well disguised. Although most of the fishes seen in the grass will be juveniles, such as of Parrotfishes and Wrasses, adult residents include Filefishes, Pipefishes, Longfins, Gobies and Eels. There is a species of Parrotfish which will only be found in seagrass areas *(Leptoscarus vaigiensis)*, and a Filefish *(Paramonacanthus barnadi)* which is seldom seen because of its wariness.

In the exposed vegetation free areas of sand and coral outcrops there are many bottom-dwelling species, Gobies being particularly numerous, often sharing their burrows with snapper-shrimp house cleaners. The layer of sand on the bottom is usually quite thin, and covers a hard substrate of old coral, which contains cracks and holes that serve as refuges for young Butterflyfishes, Picasso Triggerfishes and visitors from the fringing reef. The greatest variety of life will be found in and around the coral outcrops, where fishes form surprisingly mixed communities tolerating each other in their prime concern for security. Sea Urchins will invariably be found under and around these coral outcrops and they provide excellent protection for juvenile fishes which hide amongst their spines, in the company of the ubiquitous Cardinalfishes. The sandy areas around the coral outcrops are home for juvenile Razorfishes and Flatheads, Flounders and Soles and many other bottom dwelling fishes.

A small, football-sized head of branching coral is always worth close scrutiny. Such coral heads can be home for a large number of small fishes, in addition to the very conspicous Banded Dascyllus and Blue Green Chromis - amongst the branches may be found the delightful little red striped, green bodied Goby *(Gobiodon rivulatus)*, and at the base of the coral head an agitated Olive Dottyback will be darting in and out of cover.

Close inshore a number of silvery fishes will be encountered, often in large shoals. They are highly reflective (difficult to photograph) and always on the move. Typical of these fishes are the Mojarras, of which there are two species in the Red Sea. They will be observed taking mouthfuls of sand, which they filter to obtain the minute organisms contained in it. They are characterised by their downward pointing mouth, especially designed for this feeding style.

Monos are another of the silvery fishes seen inshore, usually in areas which snorkellers tend to avoid - they prefer low salinity areas, such as waste water outflows, and brackish areas. Mullet (two species are found in the Red Sea) will also be seen in the same environment, although it is not unusual to see large shoals of Mullet near the fringing reef, usually swimming just below the surface.

An unusual fish that a snorkeller may be fortunate to see is the Shrimpfish, *Aeoliscus strigatus*. These fishes swim in a head down attitude, and at first glance appear to be sticks suspended in the water. They are silver with a greenish hue, and have a black strip along the length of their bodies - this colouring makes them almost invisible when hiding in their preferred refuge, the long-spined black sea urchins.

Man-made structures along the coast provide sancturies for a variety of fishes; some fishes seem actually to prefer the dark maze of pipes and concrete columns

Red Sea Halfbeak *Hyporhamphus gamberur*

Size: to 20cm

Endemic to the Red Sea and Gulf of Aden. Halfbeaks will be seen swimming just below the surface, over shallow or deep water.

Lacepède 1803

Fourspot Sardine *Herklotsichthys quadrimaculatus*

Size: to 15cm

The Fourspots are the fish with the yellow stripe, and four black spots along the dorsal spine. The majority of the school shown is another, unidentified species of the Clupeidae family, or possibly of the Anchovies (Engraulididae)

Rüppell, 1837

Blacktip Mojarra *Gerres argyreus*

Size: to 23cm

Seen singly or in small groups in sheltered, shallow water. They feed by sifting sand through their downward pointing mouths.

Bloch & Schneider, 1801

found under piers. Significant amongst these fishes are the Spadefishes, Turkeyfishes and Cardinalfishes - such fishes also appear to favour wrecks and rubble areas. A discarded section of water pipe will often be home for a small Moray eel, and a soft drink can a home for a Blenny.

Shrimpfish (Centriscidae)
Aeoliscus *strigatus*

Milkfish (Chanidae)
Chanos *chanos*

Mojarra (Gerreidae)
Gerres *argyreus*
Gerres *oyena*

Mullet (Mugilidae)
Oedalechilus *labiosus*
Mugil *cephalus*
Liza *macrolepis*
Valamugil *seheli*
Crenimugil *crenilabis*

Sardine (Clupeidae)
Herklotsichthys *quadrimaculatus*

Mono (Monodactyllidae)
Monodactylis *argenteus*
Monodactylis *falciformis*

Silverside (Atherinidae)
Atherinomorus *lacunosus*

Eels
Electrophorus *electricus*
Gorgasia *sillneri*
Conger *cinereus*

Slenderspine Mojarra *Gerres oyena*

Size: to 32cm

▼ MOJARRA • Gerreidae

Similar to *G. argyreus,* but without the black on the dorsal fin.

Forsskål, 1775

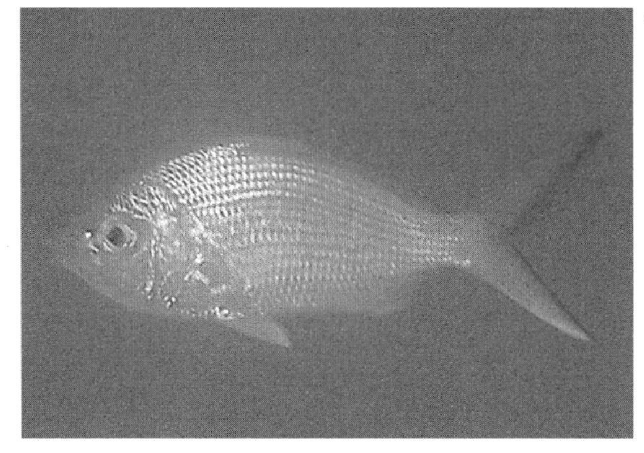

Shrimpfish *Aeoliscus strigatus*

Size: to 15cm

▼ SHRIMPFISH • Centriscidae

Swims with head vertically down over sandy bottom. Hides amongst spines of sea urchins, where its lateral stripe helps to disguise it. This species has not been reported from the Red Sea. Photographed near Jeddah.

Bianconi, 1855

Fringelip Mullet *Crenimugil crenilabis*

Size: to 60cm

▼ MULLET • Mugilidae

Swims in small schools over sandy flats and sometimes the reef tops.

Forsskål, 1775

Bibliography

Fishes of the world - An illustrated Dictionary — Alwyne Wheeler
Ferndale Editions, London. 1975 — ISBN 0-905746-05-8

Red Sea Reef Fishes — Dr. John E Randall
IMMEL Publishing, London 1983 — ISBN 0-907151-04-3

Reef Fishes of the Indian Ocean — Dr. Gerald R Allen and Roger C Steene
T.F.H. Publications Inc. — ISBN 0-86622-191-3

The Red Sea in Egypt. Part 1 — Farid S Atiya
Published by the author — ISBN 977-00-0443-X

The Red Sea — Dr. Peter Vine
IMMEL Publishing — ISBN 0-907151-10-8

A Field guide to the Coral Reef Fishes of the Indian and Pacific Oceans — R. H. Carcasson
Collins — ISBN 0-00-219664-6

Indian Ocean - Tropical Fish Guide — Helmut Debelius
ISBN 3-927991-01-5

Tropical Marinelife — Dieter Eichler
ISBN 1-89-8162107

Red Sea Explorers — Peter Vine & Hagen Schmid
IMMEL Publishing — ISBN 0-907151-30-2

An updated checklist of the Fishes of the Red Sea: CLOFRES II — Goren, M and M.Dor
International Institute for Marine Sciences, Elat.

Smith's Sea Fishes — Smith, Margaret M and Philip C Heemstra
Springer - Verlag 1986

Coral Reef Fishes - Indo-pacific & Caribbean — E Lieske & R Myers
Harper Collins — ISBN 0-00-219974-2

Coastal Fishes of OmanJ.E. Randall
Crawford House Publishing — ISBN 1-86333-126-3

Red Sea Fisheries of Sudan — William Reed
Ministry of Animal Resources, Khartoum

Papers

Aggressive mimicry and other interspecific feeding associations among Red Sea coral reef predators. — Ormond, Rupert
Journal of Zoology (London) Vol 191, 1980

Review of Indo-Pacific labrid fish genus Wetmorella. — Randall, J E
Copeia Vol 4, 1983.

The Indo-Pacific Bleniid fish genus Ecsenius — Springer, V G
Smithsonian Contributions to Zoology, Vol 465, 1988.

Revision of Indo-Pacific Groupers — Randall, J E and P C Heemstra
Indo-Pacific Fishes Vol 20, 1991.

Revision of Indo-Pacific Dartfishes. — Randall, J E and D F Hoese
Indo-Pacific Fishes Vol 7, 1985.

Review of labrid fishes of the West Indian Ocean with a description of 6 new species. — Randall, J E and M M Smith
Ichthyological Bulletin of the Smith Institute of Ichthyology Vol 45, 1982.

The Parrotfishes of the Subfamily Scarinae of the Western Indian Ocean. — Randall, J E and Robin W Bruce
Ichthyological Bulletin, Vol 47, 1983.